Choosing Your Way Through the World's Medieval Past

Anne E. Schraff

illustrated by Steven Meyers

J. Weston Walch, Publisher
Portland, Maine

Users' Guide
to
Walch Reproducible Books

As part of our general effort to provide educational materials which are as practical and economical as possible, we have designated this publication a "reproducible book." The designation means that purchase of the book includes purchase of the right to limited reproduction of all pages on which this symbol appears:

Here is the basic Walch policy: We grant to individual purchasers of this book the right to make sufficient copies of reproducible pages for use by all students of a single teacher. This permission is limited to a single teacher, and does not apply to entire schools or school systems, so institutions purchasing the book should pass the permission on to a single teacher. Copying of the book or its parts for resale is prohibited.

Any questions regarding this policy or requests to purchase further reproduction rights should be addressed to:

Permissions Editor
J. Weston Walch, Publisher
P.O. Box 658
Portland, ME 04104-0658

—*J. Weston Walch, Publisher*

1   2   3   4   5   6   7   8   9   10

ISBN 0-8251-2163-9

Contents

Introduction

On the following pages are twenty adventures, beginning with an Anglo-Saxon villager in Britain and ending with a German peasant during the Reformation. (Although some history texts place the Reformation in modern history, we have placed it in medieval history because the general attitude of the people was still influenced by medieval conditions.) Beginning with life in the rude huts of the villagers who had begun to forget the Roman past, these adventures move to the threshold of the modern world and the growing spirit of revolution.

By the process of choice, the student has the chance to experience the primitive life of the Germanic tribes, the rise of European kingdoms, and the journeys of courageous explorers across continents and oceans. The student is invited to help the daughter of a bear trainer become empress of the Byzantine Empire, stand with Charlemagne in St. Peters for his crowning, live in a castle and travel with Marco Polo, flee the terrors of the Black Death, and share the glories of the Renaissance in Florence. Although the focus is on Western civilization, there are adventures among the Mayans in Central America, in the glorious golden age of China, in the bazaars of Baghdad, with the samurai in Japan and the Mali civilization in Africa, and among the Incas of Peru. Although the student's role is fictional, all the historic details are accurate. The desperation of the English serf facing loss of his fingers for hunting in the royal forest, the excitement of the Viking sailor, and the dreams of the Arab scholar bring an exciting "you are there" quality to the study of medieval history.

This book is intended to introduce medieval history to students in a way which will make it meaningful for them. It is often hard for students to understand long-ago periods when they learn only about famous people who ruled countries. These adventures enable students to share the search for daily food, the choices of vocations, the yearning for opportunity. By becoming a medieval person, the student will make choices and experience consequences which may bring triumph or tragedy, or just a different path in life. The wrong choice may bring death from the bubonic plague, the contempt of a Chinese emperor, or death from scurvy in a becalmed sea. The right choice may bring satisfaction as an Arab physician, honor as a great goldsmith, or power at the side of the Spanish explorers.

As a supplement to the textbook, these adventures will spark the imagination of students and make distant peoples real and much like people living today. All the different traditions are treated with respect, and commonly accepted virtues of courage, honesty, compassion, and striving for excellence are highlighted.

Each adventure is supplemented with a short reading about an interesting person, event, or sidelight about the era. This material is entirely factual. There are matching or true/false questions for each reading. There are also suggestions for group and individual activities for each segment.

Other recommended activities for all the segments include the following:

- Students might keep a written record of the pages they chose and what happened to them in their adventures.

- The teacher might conduct regular discussions among groups who chose different courses of action and ask questions like "What usually guided your decision?"

- Students might be asked at the conclusion of several segments what they have learned about decision making, and their own attitudes so far. At the end of the book, these questions could be asked again to see if answers have changed.

- Vocabulary may be reviewed before each entry is read.

- At the end of the book, the class might discuss which of the civilizations or periods seemed most or least like our own. Which had the most to teach us?

- The selections do not assign a sex to any of the role-playing characters. The teacher might foster a good discussion by asking: Could all of these student characters have been either male or female? Students should be urged to get into each character, even though it appears certain that the character is of a different sex (such as a soldier in the case of a female student). All human persons share the same fears, hopes, and dreams, and this should be emphasized.

- At the end of the book students might write an essay on their favorite civilization or period, giving reasons why. What values in this civilization or period did they admire? Are these values we have lost, or never had in our society?

- At the end of the book the entire class might choose specific values or ideas they admired from various civilizations or periods.

A Germanic Villager— A.D. 500

You live in an Anglo-Saxon village in Britain. Your parents raise grains, vegetables, and fruits. You eat these foods, as well as meat from your pigs. You have an alphabet consisting of about twenty-four letters called runes. The runes have simple lines, which you carve or etch into wood, bone, or stone.

About thirty families live in your farming village. Your house is a thatched hut with one room. It is built out of wood and clay. You don't have a chimney. The smoke from your fire escapes through a hole in the roof. When the weather is cold, your cow and the pigs live in the house with you. The more creatures you have breathing in the small hut, the warmer it is.

You love to walk through your village and look at the one fine home. You like to dream that when you are grown you will live in such a house.

Today all your chores are done, and you walk down the road to look again at the fine home. As you walk, you see stone ruins. These were once Roman villas. A very old man told you of them.

The lord of the village lives in the fine home. He owns the land your parents and the others farm. The lord's house is made from split logs. It has a kitchen and separate sleeping rooms. How wonderful it must be to have a separate room to sleep in! Your brothers and sisters and even the pigs step on you as you sleep!

The lord has silver and gold ornaments that shine like the sun. You cannot imagine owning such beautiful things! You would never tire of looking at them if they were yours.

You are old enough to take some household utensils to your grandparents in the next village. They are old and cannot travel. You should leave at once, but you are tempted to delay. Sometimes the lord lets you do chores for him. Then he allows you to touch his ornaments.

■ *If you leave at once for your grandparents' village, turn to page 3.*

■ *If you stop at the lord's house, turn to page 4.*

Find out what your fate is!

You load the heavy sack filled with pliers, a chisel, some knives, and a few wooden spoons over your back. You hurry down the old Roman road. Your parents are very proud of you to be making this long journey alone.

The first night you plan to sleep under a tree because the weather is warm. But you fear being robbed during the night. You walk into a meadow and dig a hole. Here you will bury the few coins you carry. You will hide your sack in the brush.

But as you dig you strike something hard! At first you think it's a rock. After digging deeper you find a small box. You open it with trembling fingers. It is filled with silver spoons! How the silver shines! You find a big spoon, a middle-sized spoon, and a tiny pointed spoon. You remember stories your old friend in the village told you. The Romans used different spoons for everything!

You forget all about sleeping. You are too excited. You load the box into your sack and hurry towards the next village. You will be able to offer a coin to sleep in someone's hut. It will be safer there. You cannot risk being robbed of your silver spoons!

As you rush along, you meet a man coming in the opposite direction. He wears a sheepskin and an old cloak. You hope he is not a beggar. You dislike turning people down and you are much too poor to share. You don't know how much the silver spoons will bring, but you will need every bit of it for your family.

As the man draws closer, you see he is a monk.

"Good evening," you say cheerfully. He has kindly blue eyes and he wears a wooden cross around his neck. Perhaps he will give you a blessing.

"Good evening," he says. "Are you a traveler in need of a night's shelter, youngster?"

"Yes. I was going to the village," you say.

"Ah, we have a few huts for travelers up in the hills. We can offer you bread and cheese and a mat to sleep on," says the monk.

You find the offer tempting. But what if the man is not the monk he appears to be? What if he is a robber disguised as a monk?

■ *If you go with the man, turn to page 5.*

■ *If not, turn to page 6.*

3

You knock gently on the lord's door.

"Good morning, Sir," you say when he opens. "Do you have a chore I might help with?"

Thankfully the lord is in a fine mood. He grins and says, "Come in, youngster. You might sweep the floor. I will give you a coin and you might admire the ornaments you like so much."

You hurry to sweep the floor as the lord has an argument outside with his son, who is about your age. When you are finished, the lord tosses you a coin and you go to admire the ornaments. You touch the satin smoothness of the gold vessels and tell yourself you will own such beautiful things one day. Then you leave and go down the road. But you don't get far. The lord is running after you, his face red with anger. "A vessel of gold is missing from my home!" he shouts.

You are shocked. "My lord, I did not take it!" you cry.

"You and my son were the only ones near the house this morning. Do you think my own son would have robbed me? No, you ungrateful wretch. You loved the ornaments too much. Now you have robbed me," shouts the man.

"Look in my sack," you offer. "You will see I have only household goods I take to my grandparents."

The lord searches your sack, but he is not convinced. "You had time to hide the vessel in these woods! You are only a child, but old enough to be tried as a thief! Now woe to you!"

You are terror-struck. You have seen youngsters like you tried and convicted and punished savagely. You might be whipped or even lose a finger or a hand as a thief!

The angry lord has called his son to bind you and prepare you for trial. You wonder if you should make a run for it. You could hide in the woods and hope the real thief is uncovered. Perhaps that is safer than going on trial. But you don't want to run. That would make you look guilty.

■ *If you run, turn to page 7.*

■ *If you stay, turn to page 8.*

You decide to trust the monk. You follow him up a small hill to a few huts in a grove of trees. The monk shows you into one. There is only a mat on the floor and a stool to sit on. The monk brings you a crust of bread, some cheese, and a jug of cold water. You gladly eat the bread and cheese. It tastes wonderful because you are hungry.

"You may stay as long as you need to," says the monk.

You are curious about this man. "How long have you lived here?" you ask.

"Since I was seventeen. I am now forty-seven," he says.

"Surely you do not live on just bread and cheese in a rude hut? Not for all those years," you say.

"Ah, it's a joyous life. The beauty of the sunrise and bird songs awaken me."

"I have no fear of losing my property. I have nothing to lose," laughs the monk.

You sleep soundly. When dawn is red in the sky, you get up and splash cold water on your face. Then you hear singing! At this hour? You peer from your hut. Sure enough, the monks are singing as they walk up the hill!

You notice a few other huts far from the grove. When the monks stop singing you ask who lives there.

"Ah," says the monk you have met before, "that is where the lepers[1] live. They have no other place to go because people are afraid of them. We take care of them, but their huts must be a little ways from the huts we offer the travelers. The travelers would not want to be near the poor lepers."

Your heart is touched. You reach in your bag and give the monk the large silver spoon. "You may have this to sell and help the lepers."

"Bless you," says the monk.

You hurry on to the village and sell the other two spoons for a good price. Then you go to your grandparents' house. It is a happy visit. You are proud of yourself for making the long journey. And you feel good about giving away the silver spoon.

■ *Turn to page 9.*

---

[1]People suffering from the disease called leprosy. Once incurable and deforming, it was feared. Now it can be treated.

You decline the monk's offer and hurry on to the village with your sack of silver spoons and tools. You offer an old couple a coin to sleep in their hut. You sleep with the sack under your pillow. You dread that something will happen to your silver spoons.

In the morning you hurry on. When you stop for lunch, you look in your sack. Oh no! The middle-sized silver spoon is gone. You were robbed! How clever they were not even to awaken you! What light-fingered thieves!

You hurry on again until you find a wealthy shopkeeper. You show him the two silver spoons.

"I will buy the large one," he says. "I do not care for the tiny one. I think the Romans used it to eat eggs and shellfish."

You tuck the coins you received into your cloak. It is less than you expected. You are disappointed. Did the shopkeeper cheat you? How should a poor youngster like you know?

As you near your grandparents' village, you notice ragged-looking fellows behind you. You decide to run. Then you trip on a rock and your sack goes flying. The chisel and the tiny silver spoon tumble into a ravine. You cannot get them back. Oh, what miserable luck.

When you reach your grandparents' hut, they greet you warmly. They hug and kiss you. They are poor people, but they have even made a little cake for you. How good the honey cake tastes with fresh milk.

You tell your grandparents the sad story of the silver spoons. "I thought I was rich, and now I just have a few coins. I was robbed and struck with misfortune."

"Ah," says your grandmother with a little chuckle. "You had nothing before you found the silver spoons. Now you have several coins. So you are lucky. Do not count what is lost. Count only the good you have."

You remember those words all your life. You always count what is good in your life. You try to forget the bad things very quickly. You find your grandmother gave you good advice. Such advice is worth more than a dozen silver spoons!

■ *Turn to page 9.*

You run quickly into the woods. You have spent many hours roaming here. The lord and his son cannot find you because you know tree hollows and caves to hide in.

But you are an outlaw! Soon everybody thinks you stole the golden vessel. You do not dare return even to your parents' house.

You live off the land for many weeks. You keep hoping that the true thief will be found. But then an old traveler tells you that your hopes are foolish. He thinks the son of the lord himself stole the vessel and the truth will never come out. You think the same. You must flee to where nobody knows you.

You make your way to the English Channel and cross over to the other side on a keel boat, a long narrow boat propelled by oars. You arrive in Gaul, where war has been raging for a long time. There is a Frankish leader named Clovis who is trying to conquer everybody else and rule alone. Different tribes are battling all the time. You are so frightened. It is dangerous even for a youngster to travel through the countryside.

You must steal to live. You were never a thief when the lord accused you. But now you must be a thief. You snatch a chicken here and some fruit there. You are sorry to do it, but there is no other way to keep alive. You are sure that even God will forgive you for crimes like this.

You find small jobs here and there. But most of the time you must steal. Nobody will hire a skinny youngster without skills. How you long to go home, but that can never be.

One night, as you sleep in strange woods, a cold, driving rain comes. You crawl deeper under the tree, but soon you are soaking wet and shivering. Death comes to you before dawn. Now, at last, you will have peace. You have lived a short, hard life.

■ *Turn to page 9.*

You are innocent and you refuse to run. You are sure that you will be declared innocent in the trial.

Your guilt or innocence will be decided in an unusual way. It is called trial by ordeal. You are tied up and lowered into cold water. If you sink, you will be declared innocent because pure water will not receive a guilty person, it is believed. If you float, you will be declared guilty. Then you will be pulled out and punished as a thief.

You are very nervous as you plunge into the cold water. You sink at once! You almost drown before you are pulled from the water!

"Good youngster," says your accuser, the lord of the village, "I can see now that you were misjudged by me. I was wrong to accuse you. The water has proven you guiltless by accepting your innocent young body."

You are glad to be free, but you do not like the lord anymore. You smile and do chores for him, but in your heart you dislike him very much.

One day as you are walking past the lord's house, you see his son hurry by with a beautifully engraved sword. You know that is the lord's most treasured possession.

You go to the back door of the lord's house and tell him what you saw. He rushes out as the son is climbing on his horse.

"Ungrateful son!" shouts the lord. "You would steal my sword?"

"You are stingy, father. You drive me to steal," cries the wretched son.

You are surprised by what happens next. The lords takes his sword from the son. Then he turns and gives it to you! "Here, good youngster, sell this treasure for the good of your poor family! You showed me the truth about my wicked son."

The sword brings a good price. Your family can now live in a better home and have more pigs and two cows. You can even give money to your grandparents so that their lives are easier.

■ *Turn to page 9.*

Treasures of the Anglo-Saxons

The Angles and the Saxons were primitive Germanic tribes who settled in England. They were not civilized like the Romans, but they had treasures of their own. One was a poem called *Beowulf*. This poem was spoken at feasts and around fires. Then it was written down. It tells about a young hero named Beowulf who defeats an evil monster named Grendel. In the poem are strange and colorful terms. The sea is called a *whale-path*. A traveler is called an *earth-stepper*. The story is rich with excitement and drama. It has been loved for hundreds of years.

Matching

_____ 1. Letters of the Anglo-Saxon alphabet   a) Beowulf

_____ 2. The head of a village   b) runes

_____ 3. The young hero in the Anglo-Saxon poem   c) sea

_____ 4. The evil monster in the Anglo-Saxon poem   d) Grendel

_____ 5. Whale-path   e) lord

Group Activities

1. Find a copy of *Beowulf* and read portions of it aloud in class.

2. On a large map of the medieval period find the different Germanic tribes and note where they settled. Find the regions settled by the Franks, Ostrogoths, Visigoths, Vandals, Burgundians, Angles, and Saxons. What countries are these today?

3. Discuss what life was probably like for the farmer who lived on the lord's land. How would this life compare with that of migrant workers today?

Individual Activities

1. Find information about one of the following people and write one paragraph about him.

   a) Clovis   b) Venerable Bede

2. Look up runic writing. Copy a few sentences.

3. Using the type of colorful language in *Beowulf,* write a colorful term for the following:

   airplane   automobile   spacecraft
   baseball player   singer

The Girl Who Became an Empress—A.D. 526

You are the child of an innkeeper in Constantinople. An entertainer and his daughter are staying at the inn. The entertainer has performing bears. The bears do tricks in the large amphitheatre, a stadium with rows of seats around a bowl-shaped design. You are thrilled at the idea of performing bears. It amazes you that wild animals can do tricks. You must see them.

One morning you ask the entertainer's daughter if the bears really do tricks. She smiles and nods. She is very beautiful.

"Are you an entertainer, too?" you ask her.

"Yes. I am Theodora. I can dance and sing very well," she says. "But someday I want to do more important things."

"It must be exciting to perform before a lot of people," you say. As the child of an innkeeper, your life is quite interesting. You meet many different people. But there's much dull, hard work, too. You have to clean up after the guests and many are sloppy and dirty.

Theodora laughs and says, "I do not have such an exciting life now. I am very poor. I am poorer than you. I cannot wear the pretty clothes I need. You see, I want to make friends with nice people. Then I will get ahead in life. Right now I am little better off than the dancing bears. But someday I will be a great lady."

You admire Theodora's spirit. You dream of better things, too. You want to study the law. You would like to be a lawyer and advise important people. Already you have read many books and done a lot of studying. "I am pretty well educated," you say. "Maybe I could teach you some things that would help you."

Theodora's eyes light up. "Maybe we could help one another. Then when I am rich and famous I will give you a good job. Maybe I will even one day be empress!"

You are shocked. What a fantastic dream for a poor little bear trainer's daughter. You are not so sure you should get mixed up with such a dreamer!

■ *If you do help Theodora, turn to page 13.*

■ *If you don't, turn to page 14.*

Find out what your fate is!

There is something about this young woman that you like very much. She seems to be destined for great things. It seems as though she would not abuse power if she ever got it. You have a feeling she will do something wonderful someday. And you would like to be a part of it.

You help Theodora with her speech and manners. Soon she makes friends with important people. She travels around the provinces of the empire with some rich people. You go along on some of the trips. You help her learn to make clever conversation.

It's a thrill to see how Theodora is changing. She is now as clever as she is beautiful. She not only listens with great interest as you tell her about Greek classics, but she is your friend!

Now Theodora is invited to a royal banquet. You help her pick out her clothing. Your mother has graciously lent some pearls which you give to Theodora to wear.

"Do you think Emperor Justinian will notice me?" Theodora asks you.

"Emperor Justinian?" you gasp. "Is he going to be at the banquet?"

Theodora smiles. "Yes," she says, "and I have heard he is seeking a wife. I should be his wife. I was born to wear purple, the color of royalty."

You are amazed. But Theodora is determined. She is so beautiful that surely the Emperor will look at her. But would he ever marry a girl who once danced at a trick bear show?

You have never seen Justinian, but you are in awe of him. After all, he is the most powerful man in the Byzantine Empire. One word from him can make war or bring peace. Hundreds live and die by his command.

"Beware your friend's boldness," warns your father. "If the emperor thinks he is being trapped into marriage to an ambitious woman, be no part of it!"

■ *If you attend the banquet with Theodora, turn to page 15.*

■ *If not, turn to page 16.*

You wish Theodora luck, but you decide not to become a close friend. After all, to be a lawyer you must spend a lot of time studying.

When you are not cleaning rooms at the inn, you are studying the law.

Because of your learning, you are invited to join a large group of lawyers in A.D. 527. Emperor Justinian wants the whole body of Roman law to be revised. Your group is going to do it.

There are so many Roman laws now in effect. Many disagree with each other. Your task is to get rid of the bad laws that don't make sense. Then you must rewrite the good laws in simpler, fairer ways.

The work is very hard, but you and the others make great progress. By A.D. 533 you produce what is called *Corpus Juris Civilis,* or the Justinian Code.

You present your work to Emperor Justinian. What a great honor to be of such service to the Emperor and all of Rome. Emperor Justinian stands before you in a flowing purple robe. A glittering jeweled crown is on his head. "Well done, jurists [lawyers]," he says. "All the world will thank us."

But then you see a familiar face. It is Theodora, now Empress. There, draped in royal robes, pearls dangling from her shoulders, is the daughter of the bear keeper! You are sure she has seen you, for she winks!

Now you go out into the countryside to make sure the new laws are being enforced. Two interesting cases immediately come to you. You and another jurist must travel to render decisions in these cases.

"One of the cases involves a married couple fighting over the future of their son," says the other jurist. "And the other case is about an upaid debt. I will let you choose which you want to handle and I will take the other one."

■ *If you take the marriage case, turn to page 17.*

■ *If you take the debt case, turn to page 18.*

You walk into the great banquet hall. Golden goblets hold sparkling wines. Bowls overflow with delicious dark purple and green grapes. They are bursting with juicy goodness. A great savory roasted lamb sits dripping gravy on a plate. You want to start eating right away, but of course you can't.

You glance at Theodora. You thought she would be nervous. This is the big moment. She will try to meet the Emperor and become his friend. But Theodora is very cool—though you are shaking! She acts as if she is already an empress.

Suddenly a hush falls. Justinian enters wearing silk robes. You can scarcely see his face for the glow of the jewels on his crown. All men bend their knee before approaching him.

How could the bear trainer's daughter dare to approach such a man? But before the banquet is over Theodora is chatting away with the Emperor! And from that day forward, she is among his circle of friends.

In a short time Theodora has won the heart of the Emperor. She becomes Justinian's wife. And you are chosen as a close adviser. You are now an important part of the Byzantine Empire's government. Theodora kept her promise to you.

In A.D. 532 there is an uprising in the empire. Mobs are in revolt against Justinian. Theodora comes to you with shocking news. "Justinian speaks of fleeing the city! He sees the torches of revolution lighting up the night sky and he loses his courage! You must come with me and stand by me when I convince him to stand firm," Theodora says.

You go to the royal chambers. It is Theodora who speaks most of the time though. "Exile is impossible! We have been born to the purple and we never flee before a mob," she cries in a passionate voice.

You try to point out to Justinian that the revolt can be controlled by the loyal soldiers. But it is Theodora who convinces him. He fights the revolt and wins. You smile in wonder at the beautiful Empress. She is as much the ruler of the Byzantine Empire as he is—perhaps more so.

■ *Turn to page 19.*

You dare not attend the banquet with Theodora. She is much too bold. She will surely get in trouble and you will be hurt too.

When Theodora must go alone, your friendship with her suffers. You are never close again. But still you are happy for her when she become Empress. You know she will make a wonderful wife for Justinian. You are sorry you lacked the courage to go to the banquet with her. You would have liked to share her triumph.

Now you study the law. Justinian has issued a new law code. As a lawyer it is up to you to work with the new law. You are called upon to defend a man accused of being disloyal to the emperor. At a public function he did not lie face down before the emperor as the law said he must.

"The fellow deserves death," shouts the accusing lawyer. "He must be made an example of. If respect for the Emperor breaks down, our whole society will fall apart. He must be taken to the stadium and executed so all will know we must show respect to Justinian!"

You search the new Justinian Code to find something to help the accused man. You believe he did not mean to show disrespect to the Emperor. He just didn't see why he had to lie face down when his knees hurt. He was afraid he couldn't get up again if he did that.

"Our great Emperor Justinian," you argue, "provides mercy even for offenses such as this. Justinian's code says that a fine may be imposed instead of death. The fine will be used to help the state, but the death of the man will help no one."

You win and the man gets off with a fine. You will use the Justinian Code in many such cases. Although it is stern in many ways, it is the most fair code that you have ever seen.

You are sure that the gentle hand of Theodora may be seen in the most compassionate of provisions! (Especially those about women!)

■ *Turn to page 19.*

You go to the villa where the married couple live. They say they are happily married, but they cannot agree on the future of their son.

"Our son is destined for great power and leadership," says the father. "Like me, he will do well in a military career. He will be a clever general giving great service to the empire. I could predict this even when he was a small child walking so tall and straight."

"This is not what our son wants," says the mother. "He is a gentle boy with an artistic spirit. Ever since he was very young he showed great skill with his hands. He likes to work with mosaics [small cubes of glass or stone], and the pictures he makes are a wonder to see."

You look at the two people. It is clear that they love one another. But this issue is dividing them. The boy they are fighting about is a handsome child. His eyes are full of confusion. It makes him unhappy to see his parents fighting over him. He tells you he would like to make icons (Christian religious pictures), but he will do anything to keep the peace. You ask the boy, "You really do not want to be a soldier then, do you?"

"No. But I will do as I am told like a dutiful son," says the boy.

You go to the father then. "Your son wants to be an artist. This is where his heart is."

The father grows very angry. "It does not matter what the boy wants. He must do what I say. I am the father. Roman law is clear. Absolute power in the rearing of children is with the *pater familias* [father of the family]."

"Yes, that's how it used to be," you say, "but according to the new law, the Justinian Code, the mother has equal authority. So if your wife wants to permit the boy to be an artist, she may. And the boy does not break the law in disobeying you."

The boy and his mother seem very happy. You are glad to have used the new code to help. You are sure that the Empress Theodora had a hand in preparing this law!

■ *Turn to page 19.*

You come upon a poor fellow who cannot pay for a goat he purchased. He promised the goat herder to pay, but then he lost his job. His family has eaten the goat. And now he has nothing left to pay the goat herder.

"Imprison him," shouts the goat herder. "The scoundrel must be cast into prison and beaten. If he still does not pay, then let us have his hand chopped off because he is a thief! He took my goat and now does not pay, which is the same as if he had stolen my goat."

You look at the poor, cowering man. "I wanted to do the right thing. But my family and I were hungry. If I had found another job I would have paid for the goat. Please do not throw me in prison. How can I look for work if I am in prison? And if my hand is chopped off, then I can never find work at all," he says.

You consult the new Justinian Code. There is a provision here for a case such as this. You call the goat herder and the accused man and tell them. "The debt shall be written down. Jailing the debtor is useless. Every effort must be made to find work for the debtor. Out of his first wages the debt must be paid."

The goat herder is very angry. He wants the poor debtor punished. But the law is the law.

The man who took the goat soon gets a job sweeping the streets. He pays his debt with his first wages even though his family has only dry bread and water to eat.

"You see," you tell the goat herder, "the new code works. If your cruel command had been carried out, the poor man would have no hand. And you would not have your money. Do you see how wise our Emperor is?"

The goat herder must agree.

■ *Turn to page 19.*

The Walls of Constantinople

Constantinople was a rich and powerful city. Three sets of walls were built to protect it from invaders. It also had a moat (a canal) sixty feet wide and twenty feet deep. The walls had ninety-six towers used by armed soldiers who watched for enemies. Sadly, the Byzantine Empire did not enjoy much peace in spite of the walls. It was attacked by Goths, Huns, Persians, Bulgars, Slavs, and many others. And then the beautiful city itself was attacked and looted in 1204 by Crusaders. They were supposed to be fighting to protect holy places, but instead they broke into Constantinople and left it in ruins.

Matching

_____ 1. Number of walls built to defend Constantinople   a) Justinian

_____ 2. Theodora's father's job   b) bear trainer

_____ 3. The person Theodora married   c) three

_____ 4. Stadium with rows of seats shaped like a bowl   d) Crusaders

_____ 5. Who finally attacked and looted Constantinople   e) amphitheatre

Group Activities

1. Discuss what kind of personality you think Theodora had. What famous women would you compare her with today? If Theodora were alive today, do you think she would be plotting to marry a powerful man, or would she dream of something else?

2. Discuss an appropriate punishment for the following crimes:

   a) Spraying graffiti on a storefront
   b) Stealing five dollars
   c) Punching a friend during an argument

3. Discuss whether or not Justinian was a good ruler. What makes a good ruler?

Individual Activities

1. Using colored stones, make a simple mosaic.

2. There is a famous mosaic of Emperor Justinian and Empress Theodora. Find a picture of it in a history book. Then, in one paragraph, describe the mosaic.

3. The Byzantine Empire used a terrible weapon called Greek fire. Find out what it was, and write two paragraphs about it.

The Mayan Adventure— A.D. 600

You are a young Mayan in Central America. You live in a warm forest with clearings where maize grows. Your house is a pole and thatch hut.

Often you go to ceremonial centers to attend festivals. You dress simply, wearing woven cotton garments which are cool in this hot climate. You enjoy eating roast turkeys and ducks as well as squash, beans, and chili peppers to flavor everything.

This morning you are on your way to a festival. You look forward to the colorful event, and you are not disappointed when you get there. The ceremonial center is a great temple on a pyramid platform. Steep stairs lead up. You will not go up the stairs though. You will watch from the square below as a few chosen people carry gifts up the stairs.

Some musicians carry long trumpets, which they blow. The sound echoes all around the woodland. Other musicians carry rattles and drums. Then the dancers come. They wear large crablike claws on their arms and hands. Some wear long-nosed masks which remind you of birds. You like the jaguar masks best. They are very scary! They look so real you can almost hear them snarl!

The people carry gifts up the stairs. They carry beans, squash seeds, flowers, and sweet-smelling incense. They will offer these to the spirits of the Mayan gods for a good harvest.

After the festival you head back to your village. You have talked to many friends and feasted. But you are eager to get home because great clouds gather overhead. You don't want to be caught out in a storm, because the rivers overflow quickly.

You reach home before the rains fall, but the next day it is still cloudy. You had planned to journey through the jungle to trade some rubber for vanilla. Is it dangerous to travel in this stormy weather? You have done it before, but today the clouds look very dark.

■ *If you go anyway, turn to page 23.*

■ *If not, turn to page 24.*

Find out what your fate is!

You put your rubber in a sack and swing the sack over your shoulder. The rubber is in the form of orange-sized balls. Children and young people like to play games with the balls. You made the rubber balls by first collecting a white liquid that oozes from certain trees. You let the liquid dry and boiled it in water. Then you formed balls.

The rain is falling lightly as you head into the thick jungle towards another village. Your village needs vanilla especially to make a delicious chocolate and vanilla drink. Everybody likes it. You cannot imagine anything else that tastes as good.

As you hurry along, splashing in the marshes in your bare feet, you see strong vines ahead. You grab one and swing gracefully over a river. Usually the river is very slow moving. Now it is swollen with rainwater and it rushes swiftly along.

You sail over the river with your sack of rubber. Then you continue on your way as a bright blue parrot shrieks at you.

Suddenly a spotted yellow jaguar leaps into the path straight ahead. The jaguar has chased some howler monkeys up a tree. Now the clever monkeys swing to safety on the vines across the tops of the trees. The jaguar has lost his lunch! But he is still hungry and he casts his gaze on you!

You enjoyed watching the people with the jaguar masks at the festival. But this is a real jaguar, large and dangerous. Has he ever eaten a person? If so, he is twice as dangerous. You see vines hanging all around. Should you follow the example of the howler monkeys and try to swing to safety in the trees? You are very agile.

Or should you clamber up a nearby tree? Maybe the jaguar would lose interest in you then.

■ *If you climb a tree? turn to page 25.*

■ *If you swing on the vines, turn to page 26.*

You decide to wait for better weather. You sit in your hut and listen to the rain pour down on the canopy of trees. To pass time you work on some pottery. You are a good potter and artist. You paint a Mayan chief holding a spear. Your father is very impressed with your painting.

"You have painted the chief with a fine, sloping forehead. It is handsome work," says your father.

"You are very clever," your mother says, turning the beautiful pot around in her hands.

"There is a merchant coming here tomorrow. Perhaps he will take this pot and others you have painted on the caravan. We might receive cotton cloth or chocolate beans in exchange," says your father.

You have often thought of going on a trade caravan yourself. You think it would be exciting. But you would be gone from your village for many months. It is a big decision.

"Perhaps I could go on the trade caravan this time," you say.

"You are a big help to us in the village," says your father.

"Some trade caravans are unlucky. You could be swept away into a roaring river or killed by wild animals," says your mother.

"Sometimes I wonder what is beyond this village," you say. "Is the world far different down the road?"

You think about your plans for a long time. You climb to the highest spot in your village, atop a tall tree. You see hills and mountains in the distance. You wonder if the mountains look different when you get right up to them. Are there entirely different kinds of animals there?

One day you are eager to go, and the next you are afraid. And then, finally, it is time to decide.

■ *If you go on the trade caravan, turn to page 27.*

■ *If not, turn to page 28.*

You scramble up the tree and the jaguar prowls below. You can almost see him licking his mouth as he dreams of eating you!

The rain has stopped and you cling to the branch until the jaguar gets tired and looks for something else to eat. You come down the tree then and continue your journey.

When you reach the other village, the young people gather around you to see your rubber balls. You spend a little time bouncing the balls back and forth in an instant game. It is a lot of fun.

A Mayan youth about your age comes up and says, "I know the art of numbers. Do you know?"

"I have heard of such a thing, but I know nothing about it," you say.

"You see," says the youth, kneeling in the dirt with a pointed stick, "I will write here how many balls you brought in your sack."

You watch in fascination as the youth scratches a bar-shaped sign in the dirt. "This is the sign for five." Then he makes four dots. "Now we have the bar which means five and four dots. That is a total of nine."

"What if I had twice as many balls as I have. How would you write that?" you ask.

The youth draws three bars and three dots atop them in the dirt. "This is how eighteen is written."

You smile. "What if I had as many balls as I have fingers on both my hands?" you ask.

The youth draws two bars in the dirt.

When you return to your village, you cannot wait to share your new knowledge. You bring the vanilla you traded for the rubber balls. Then you say, "I bring something even better! Listen and watch!"

Soon many gather around you as you kneel on the dirt and draw bars and dots. You are so proud you can write numbers!

■ *Turn to page 29.*

You grab the vines and swing over a rushing river. You land well beyond the hungry jaws of the jaguar. He will not get you today. But as you swung, the sack with the rubber balls fell into the river. Now you have nothing to trade for the vanilla you need.

You kneel at the edge of the river. You see your knotted sack in the middle of the water. It has been snagged by a jagged uprooted tree that is lodged in the river.

You must somehow get the sack. You cannot return to your village with neither the rubber balls nor the vanilla.

The rain has stopped as you reach into the river with a long branch. You almost, but not quite, can reach your sack. You must swim into the murky water!

You enter the river and try swimming towards the sack. But the current is so powerful! You never dreamed it could be like this! You are like a leaf swept along. Oh! You will surely be dashed to death on a rock!

Faster and faster you go, swirling and bobbing in the rushing river. Why does the water go so fast? The land beside the river is thick with vines and trees. You have never been here before. Where are you going?

Suddenly the river plunges into a misty falls! You are hurled over the edge, down, down. This is the end! You cannot believe such a misfortune is happening to you.

By some miracle you are still alive in the water below. Soaked and bruised, you crawl onto marshy land. You start the long walk home. You dread the anger of your parents. You have lost the rubber balls and have no vanilla!

But when you finally arrive home you are amazed. Everybody begins to scream and dance around with joy.

"Look who is back from the land of the dead," cries your sister.

Everybody is so happy to see you alive that they forget to be angry at all!

■ *Turn to page 29.*

You go on the trade caravan. Porters carry the goods to be traded, and men armed with spears walk alongside. You walk with the merchants, your heart racing with excitement. You are doing something you never did before.

You soon come to a great city filled with temples and pyramids. You never dreamed such a place existed. The pyramids are much bigger than the one at the ceremonial center where you attended the festivals. These pyramids have many more steps and terraces, or platforms, going up their sides. You stare at the wonderful plaza filled with merchants exchanging pottery and cloth. You see many objects you have not seen before, like beautiful jewelry and orange pottery.

You grow tired as the caravan rises from the lowlands and climbs into the hills. You pass through many elaborate cities and small villages. How much bigger the world is than you thought!

One day you arrive at a city during a great festival. You see something that you have heard of, but never seen. You see a human being sacrificed today so that good luck will come to the people. You are frightened but very curious.

The person who will be sacrificed is tied to a wooden frame. Then warriors throw spears at him until he is struck in the heart and killed. It is a horrifying sight you will never forget.

The caravan then moves down to the seacoast. Many merchants gather here to trade. Canoes come from distant places and you see more pottery and carved stones than you have ever seen before. You enjoy the give and take of trading. You love to get something better than what you traded away. You are a good bargainer.

You will never again be content to live in your small village. You want to do this kind of work all your life.

■ *Turn to page 29.*

You decide it would be too dangerous to go on the trade caravan. Besides, you are soon interested in something else. You have become interested in looking at the skies and learning the secrets there. A wise old man in the village knows a lot about this and he teaches you. You look through a pair of crossed sticks and carefully note the way the sun and the planets change position. You enjoy watching the moon and seeing how the shape of the moon is always changing. What does this mean? Why is the moon in a different place in the sky each time you look?

"I can tell when the moon will darken completely," you tell your brother excitedly.

"Nobody can tell such a thing," your brother says with a laugh.

But you have learned to predict eclipses. Many in the village think you are a magician when you tell them when the moon will darken and it happens as you said.

You are delighted in your growing knowledge of the skies. You leave your village and go to live at a major temple. You become an advisor to the Mayan rulers. You direct stonecutters at the temple to build carved stelae which are 30-foot-high stone slabs that describe astronomical facts.

You watch the skies and see the planet Venus. You focus on Venus all the time and chart the planet's movement.

You continue this work all your life. It is never dull or boring to you. Sometimes when you return to the village where you were born, your old friends think you are strange. Why would anybody want to study the moon and the planets, they ask. They do not understand that it is the life you love.

Over a thousand years later people will marvel at what you did. They will look at the great stone slabs and say the Mayans must have been a clever people.

■ *Turn to page 29.*

Mayan Books

In the Mayan civilization there was a type of book. The book was a continuous strip of tree bark beaten flat. After the tree bark was flattened, it was coated with smooth plaster. One book was 11 feet long. It was folded into 78 pages. Then symbols, called hieroglyphics, were written on it, and illustrations were drawn. The book told about astronomy and how to predict the future.

Matching

_____ 1. Where the Mayan civilization was centered

_____ 2. What the most common Mayan garments were made of

_____ 3. What Mayan books were made from

_____ 4. What one of the Mayan books told about

_____ 5. What people came to ceremonial centers for

a) cotton

b) astronomy

c) Central America

d) festivals

e) bark

Group Activities

1. Do research on the Mayan numerical system and make a large poster illustrating it. Show the bars, dots, and shell that represented numbers 1 to 19 and 0.

2. On a large map find the Mayan empire in the New World. What countries were included?

3. Discuss the Mayan civilization. What do you think it was like to live there?

Individual Activities

1. Make drawings or models of Mayan pyramids.

2. Find out what happened to the Mayans. Are there Mayan people in the world today? Write two paragraphs to answer this question.

3. Find samples of Mayan hieroglyphics in a good encyclopedia under Mayan Civilization or History of Writing. On a small strip of tree bark, made smooth with a layer of clay, write some of these hieroglyphics.

When Charlemagne Ruled—A.D. 800

CHARLEMAGNE

It is Christmas day and you travel to Rome with Charlemagne and a large group. You are a young ambassador. Your job is to travel around the world for Charlemagne. Now you enter the Basilica of St. Peters and look around at the spacious, sunny church. There is a long row of Corinthian columns and a beautiful high altar.

Usually you live at Aachen in the western part of Germany. This is where Charlemagne lives in his palace.

Now Charlemagne kneels in prayer. He is over six feet tall. His once blonde hair and beard are grayed now with age. His handsome face is calm.

Suddenly Pope Leo III comes and places a crown on Charlemagne's head. St. Peters rings to the happy cries of the people inside. You shout along with them, "Life and victory to Charles Augustus, crowned of God, great and peace-bringing emperor!"

Charlemagne is now officially the Emperor of the Roman Empire in the West. What an important man you work for. How proud you are.

As you return with the other Franks to Aachen, you look forward to serving Charlemagne even more effectively.

Charlemagne does not act like a haughty ruler. He is kind and considerate to those who work for him. Now he calls you to the palace and says, "My faithful ambassador, I have two tasks which are very important. I wish to send you on one. You may choose. One is an errand to deliver help to poor Christian communities in the eastern part of the empire. Many of them are starving. I know I can trust you to put the money where it will do the most good. I also need someone to go to the countryside to investigate a local official who has been accused of taking bribes. To get at the truth will require courage and cleverness."

■ *If you go to the Christian communities in the East, turn to page 33.*

■ *If you investigate the local official, turn to page 34.*

Find out what your fate is!

You are glad to carry help to the poor in the Christian communities in the East. You know that Charlemagne also has a warm friendship with the King of Persia. So you will stop at his palace to offer good wishes as well.

You travel to Syria and find a small group of Christians living at the edge of the desert. You give them alms, gifts to the poor from Charlemagne. You spend some time with them before you go on to Egypt to distribute the rest of your gifts. Now it is time to visit the King of Persia. In the past, the King of Persia has sent robes, spices, and even elephants as gifts to Charlemagne.

The people of Persia follow the teachings of a prophet named Mohammed who lived two hundred years ago. They call themselves Islamic. You get along fine with them. You visit a Persian bazaar and then watch ships sailing for China loaded with camphor, copper, amber, and rhinoceros horn. You are told by a friendly Persian that the rhinoceros horn is a medicine to be used in case of poisoning.

There has been much fighting between the Christian and Islamic people. But Charlemagne gets along with Persia. You wish Charlemagne got along as well with other people. Right now he is fighting the Saxons in northern Germany and the Slavs in central Europe, as well as others. Charlemagne wants peace, but it seems there is always war!

You have a pleasant visit with the King of Persia, who is very warm and intelligent. You take part in a fine feast at the palace.

When you return to Aachen, Charlemagne praises your errand. Unfortunately you do not feel very well. You have picked up a fever which weakens you, and you would like to do easier work for a while. Since you are well educated, you could be a teacher at Charlemagne's palace, or you could spend some time copying manuscripts.

■ *If you choose to teach, turn to page 35.*

■ *If you decide to copy manuscripts, turn to page 36.*

You travel to the countryside to investigate a local count in Germany. In Charlemagne's empire each county is governed by a count. Under him are deputies, viscounts, and other local officials. The count is appointed by the king. Then the count appoints all the others.

You meet with one of the deputies and he speaks nervously. "The count here does not serve Charlemagne," he says in little more than a whisper. "He serves himself. He appoints his relatives to most jobs. The worst thing is that he takes bribes."

You wonder if this is all the truth. Sometimes a deputy will just be angry at the count for having more power than he does. You decide to check up on the way justice has been handled here.

You find a craftsman who made a pair of boots for a viscount. He delivered the boots and then was not paid. "I looked for justice in the courts. But the viscount is the nephew of the count. So the decision went against me. I was out a pair of boots and out the money due me as well," says the craftsman.

You find a woman whose son was severely punished for attacking another youth. The woman tells you sadly, "My son was going down the road when he was attacked by another youth. The other boy tried to murder my son. But the other boy swore it was my son who started the fight. I am only a poor widow so I could not bribe the count. The other boy's father is wealthy. He bribed the count and so the court decided against my son. He was cruelly flogged."

You are convinced that the charges against the count are true. But a sense of fair play tells you you must hear the count's side of the story. Only then will you be able to wholeheartedly suggest that he be fired by Charlemagne. Yet, is it dangerous to confront this count? What if he sees that you are a threat to his job and does violence to you? Maybe it would be wiser to forget fair play and hurry back to Aachen with what you already know.

■ *If you see the count, turn to page 37.*

■ *If not, and you return directly to Aachen, turn to page 38.*

You begin teaching at the palace school. You meet the great scholar Alcuin of York. You spend a whole day just listening to him.

You then begin teaching grammar, speech, and handwriting. You find the work very pleasant as you slowly get back your strength after your illness.

One day you are surprised to see Charlemagne himself enter your classroom. It is late in the day and your regular students have gone. You think perhaps Charlemagne wants to ask you how your teaching is going. But instead Charlemagne says, "I have been learning rhetoric [art of speaking] and dialectic [art of reasoning] and astronomy from Alcuin. But he has been away. I respect your knowledge. May I continue my education with you?"

You are amazed at the great Emperor's humility. He is willing to learn from you!

After you discuss the course of the stars for a while, Charlemagne tells you something that really surprises you. "You know, my good mother urged me to learn to read and I did. But I cannot really write well. I need much more help in my writing."

You try to hide your surprise. A smile comes to Charlemagne's face and he says, "I am afraid I was too busy leading my armies against the Saxons and the Slavs to learn to write well. Now, late in my life, I am trying to master the art of handwriting. I always keep tablets and writing sheets under the pillows of my couch so I can practice writing in my spare time. It is most difficult for a man my age."

You try to help Charlemagne with his writing. He never makes much progress though. But he can express himself in speech in a wonderful way. He can speak Latin and Greek, plus his own native German.

What a privilege it is to teach in Charlemagne's school—and to teach the Emperor himself! It is something you will tell your children and grandchildren.

■ *Turn to page 39.*

35

You decide copying manuscripts would be restful work until you regain your strength. The only way to make a copy of a book in your day is to copy it by hand. Otherwise there would be just one book of each kind in the world.

You learn the art of manuscript copying from a monk. For a while you work in the scriptorium, a room in the monastery built for copying manuscripts.

"Oh, what beautiful illustrations in this book," you remark.

"Ah," says the monk, "the illumination. The pictures are what we call illumination. They help those who cannot read the words. Most, you know, cannot read at all, but they can gain something by looking at the pictures."

Little by little you learn the art of illumination. At first you just decorate the first letter on the page. The first letter on your page is a *T*. You draw a huge *T* and surround it with crowns and circles and tiny pictures (called miniatures) from the life of Christ. A person who cannot read this page can see pictures of Christ as a boy working as a carpenter.

The main color you use is minium, which is a red pigment made from lead. You also use rich greens and blues and golds.

It is painstaking work, but how beautiful the results are! You grow very good at designing borders. You draw plants and flowers and geometric patterns, circles, triangles, and squares.

During the year you spend recovering your health, you can only finish a part of a book. But you are very proud of what you have accomplished. The very book you work on will last hundreds of years. It will be admired by thousands of people who see it under a glass in Rome.

■ *Turn to page 39.*

You go to the home of the count. You must choose your words carefully so he does not suspect you of having made up your mind against him. You have heard he is greedy and ruthless.

"Good count," you say, "I have been sent to look into accusations of injustice in the county. But I am sure you will be able to explain everything to my satisfaction."

"Accusations against me are false and made by jealous men," says the count. "And evildoers who did not want to pay the price for their misdeeds." A smile comes to the man's lips (though it does not make him look more pleasant). "You look intelligent and I can see you have already guessed as much."

"Well, I am looking at all sides of the issue," you explain.

"Come into my home," says the count. "My good wife and I are sitting down to a simple meal and we would be delighted if you would share it with us."

As you sit down, the count's wife brings bread, cheese, and wine.

"The grapes were bountiful in past years, so we have excellent wine," the count says.

You enjoy the food and then the count says, "If you would speak favorably of me to Charlemagne, I would be most grateful. I am a wealthy man. I would not thank you with words alone."

He is trying to bribe you! Your last doubt is gone. But you must not show that in your face. You smile and continue eating. Then the count pours you fresh wine from another bottle. As you sip, he says, "I knew from your face that you were offended by my offer of money. A person who cannot be bribed is a dangerous troublemaker."

You feel dizzy! You try to get up, but you stagger and fall. You have been poisoned! You try to reach the door, but you cannot make it. The poison was deadly. The count buries you in his garden, and Charlemagne never knows what happened to you.

■ *Turn to page 39.*

You dare not see the count. You have been told he is ruthless against his enemies. So you hurry to Aachen to tell Charlemagne what you have learned. Charlemagne listens. Anger narrows his eyes. "The scoundrel!" he shouts. "In my name he works injustice against poor and helpless people! There is no greater crime. It is treason to the welfare of the people."

The wicked count is arrested and put on trial. Justice is stern. He is executed for his crimes. There is a new just man put in his place swiftly. You are pleased that a cruel burden has been lifted from the people.

You travel all around the empire investigating complaints and making sure Charlemagne knows what's going on.

Then, one day you hear sad news. Charlemagne has been hunting. Suddenly he was struck by a sharp fever. You and many others hurry to the palace to be with your sick king.

Charlemagne lies in bed fasting. He will only take water. He believes this will cure him. But on the seventh day of his illness, he calls for a priest. He takes Holy Communion. He receives the last rites of his church. Then Charlemagne dies.

You feel such grief. Charlemagne has ruled for 47 years. He was already ruling when your father was a young man.

Charlemagne is buried the same day he dies, and you attend the burial. Then you begin to serve Louis the Pious, son of Charlemagne.

Unfortunately, you soon see how weak Louis is compared to Charlemagne. You miss the old Emperor—so does the whole empire. But the worst is yet to come. The sons of Louis the Pious are even worse. They fight among themselves so fiercely that the whole empire is torn apart.

■ *Turn to page 39.*

■ *Turn to page 39.*

The Grandsons of Charlemagne

When Louis the Pious (the son of Charlemagne) died, he left three sons. They all fought among themselves for powers. Their fighting turned into many bloody wars. Each son wanted all the land of the Western Roman empire. After all the fighting was over, Charles the Bald won the Kingdom of the West Franks (roughly France). Louis the German won the Kingdom of the East Franks (roughly Germany), and Lothair got some land in between (roughly The Netherlands, Belgium, and Luxembourg). The great kingdom of Charlemagne was forever broken up. Hundreds of years later, wars were fought between France and Germany, arising from the divisions made by the grandsons of Charlemagne.

Matching

_____ 1. The son of Charlemagne

_____ 2. Grandson who got The Netherlands

_____ 3. Grandson who got France (Kingdom of the West Franks)

_____ 4. Grandson who got Germany (Kingdom of the East Franks)

_____ 5. Where Charlemagne was crowned king.

a) Lothair

b) Louis the German

c) Rome

d) Louis the Pious

e) Charles the Bald

Group Activities

1. Many historians believe the divisions of territory among Charlemagne's three grandsons have led to modern wars. Discuss this after checking a history book and finding how many wars have been fought between Germany and France in the last one hundred years.

2. Make a large poster showing the script called Caroline Minuscule. This type of writing developed under Charlemagne. You can find samples of it in the *Random House Encyclopedia*, 1977 edition, p. 873, or *Europe in the Middle Ages*, Robert S. Hoyt, 1957 edition, p. 148, or in any large encyclopedia under Caroline Minuscule.

3. Charlemagne, great as he was, couldn't write. Is that a problem among adults today? Discuss illiteracy in America and ways everybody can help.

Individual Activities

1. Make an illustrated manuscript page such as could be found in Charlemagne's time. Just decorate the first letter as beautifully as you can.

2. Find and copy Charlemagne's autograph. You can find it on page 527 of the *New Book of Knowledge,* 1974, Volume A, or under Autographs in a large encyclopedia.

3. Read part of the *Song of Roland.* It is one of the most famous stories of the Charlemagne era.

Life in the Golden Age of China—A.D. 846

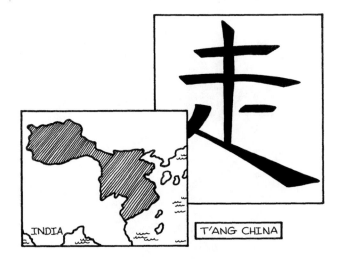

You are a young poet in China. You are just starting out. This is a golden age in China. It is the T'ang period and there is much learning and economic growth. Printing has been invented in China. What a great time to be young and full of dreams as you are!

You live in Changan (now known as Sian). Your city is square and walled. It is crossed by many tree-lined avenues. There are a million people in Changan. Your grandfather has said it must be the largest city in the whole world.

Many of your friends were not born here. They come from different parts of China and Asia. These friends are bubbling over with new ideas which they love to share with you.

One of your new friends has been to India to study Buddhism. She has brought back exciting tales of India. Another friend tells you of new ways of eating and drinking.

"Drinking tea is most pleasant," your friend says. At meals your family has always drunk wine made from rice. Now you try tea and it is delicious.

At home you sit on mats, but in your friends' homes you sometimes sit on chairs made from fine wood.

Your mind has become a mixture of rich traditional Chinese ways and exciting new ideas.

But now you wonder what sort of poems you should write. "Mother," you ask, "what should my poetry be about?"

"Write of nature," your mother advises. "Write of shadows on still ponds and the flash of color a bird makes." Your mother is very artistic. She paints the most delicate flowers and birds on vases.

"Write about the life of people," your father says. "Write poetry about the joys and sorrows of people. Such themes are lasting."

You love all kinds of poetry, but you want to focus on one special kind. Then you will be famous for that kind of poem.

■ *If you write nature poems, turn to page 43.*

■ *If you write poems about people, turn to page 44.*

Find out what your fate is!

You read the poems of Ch'u Yuan, especially "The Great Summons." He is perhaps China's most important poet. But you want to find your own voice. You want to see as much of the world as possible so you can write poetry with rich images.

A friend of your father's is a merchant and you decide to travel with him for half a year. You will pay close attention to everything you see and then your mind will overflow with ideas for your poetry.

You are soon traveling across fertile plains filled with teeming villages. A foreign merchant passes by with oxen pulling his cart. How tired the oxen look. You pity the poor brutes. You would like to write a poem describing the weariness of oxen. But this is not nature poetry.

Soon you move through a great forest. It is full of lions and bears, lynx and stags. You see one great stag in particular and you cry out, "Oh! I will make a nature poem of him surely. That beautiful creature would inspire the dullest of poets to write words that sing!"

That night you stay at a hotel. You meet a pleasant young man who is on his way to a temple. "I am devoting myself to the study of Buddhism. I am so weary of the confusion of the world," he says.

You listen as the young man speaks about his failures in life. "Now I go to examine myself. I must discover what is in my own heart," he says.

In the morning you travel past a sparkling lake. The lake and sky fill with quail, ducks, and geese. What splendid birds! You want to write about them. But you remember what the young man said. Should you first discover what is in your heart, too?

Should you explore philosophy before becoming a poet?

■ *If you start writing poetry at once, turn to page 45.*

■ *If you study philosophy first, turn to page 46.*

You decide to write about people. But first you must go to the center of the city and mix with many people. Up until now you have led a sheltered and lucky life. You want to see people not as lucky as you are.

You travel to the marketplace. People throng around the fruit stalls. You see huge pears weighing ten pounds! And what a smell! It's heavenly. The peaches are yellow and white. You can taste their sweet juiciness just by looking at them.

Suddenly you see a small child in rags. Her mother is blind. The child holds her mother by the hand. The child looks at the giant pear. You can see how she longs for some fruit. In a quiet voice she asks her mother if they might buy a pear. Her mother shakes her head. Then the child leads her mother away from the fruit stalls.

How sad it is. You wish you had thought to buy a peach or a pear for the poor child. But now the girl and her mother have vanished in the crowd.

You move on to a stall where fresh, plump fish are for sale. The wealthy are buying many fish which they will eat at one meal.

Oh! Where is that fragrance coming from? You turn to see a woman, heavily perfumed. She is dressed in beautiful silk clothing. Many servants attend her. She must live in one of the stately mansions with the wonderful gardens at the edge of the city. She must be the wife of a nobleman or great businessman.

How different is the life of the poor from such a life. The babies of the poor may be found dying by the roadside. The poor parents have nothing for them. Your heart aches for them.

Yes, you will write poems of compassion about suffering people. But is that enough? Surely your poems will touch people's hearts, and perhaps that will bring change for the good. But perhaps you ought to become a civil servant, too, and help the poor in that way. Then you could write poetry on the side.

■ *If you decide to become a civil servant, turn to page 47.*

■ *If you just write poetry, turn to page 48.*

You begin to write poems about the beauty of nature. You write about the flight of the migrating birds and the sadness when a mated pair is parted. Your mother weeps when you read her some of your poetry.

Your poems come to the attention of a very important man in the city. He invites you to a great banquet he is giving to honor his son's marriage. You read your poetry while the man's wife and daughter-in-law weep softly. Even the important man dabs at his eyes occasionally. The newly married son tells you he has been deeply moved by your poetry.

You enjoy the delicacies at the rich man's table. The fruit bowls overflow with juicy red apples, sweet dates, and pistachios. You have never tasted such delicate, crispy fish.

After the banquet you stroll in the lovely gardens with the unmarried children of the rich man. They are your age. You like them very much.

"Ah, look at the francolin—that black and white bird with the red beak," says one of the sons. "Now that is a bird worthy of a poem of his own!"

"Yes," you agree. You sit down at once on a garden bench and jot down some verse. It is not very good. Still, the new young friends you have made praise it. They are delighted by your talent.

In the spring, you find a spouse from among the rich man's children. You will now live an even more privileged life.

Your life is interesting and good. You write poetry and watch your children grow. Sometimes you travel, which you enjoy very much. And your poetry becomes more and more famous. Your life is devoted to pleasure and beauty.

Once in a while you wish you could have done something to make the world better for the poor of China. But then you write another poem and you try to forget. Most of the time you succeed.

■ *Turn to page 49.*

You go to a Buddhist study center and read the words of Buddha and other philosophers. Some of the ideas touch your heart. Some you do not understand. You are told to be a help to the sick and the hungry and to have concern for the poor. You understand that.

You spend a year of study and you come away a different person. Your parents are very surprised at the change in you.

"What has happened to you?" your mother asks. "You are so thin and pale."

"I was too busy studying to eat much food," you say. "But oh, how those ideas filled my mind. I will not only be a poet. I will use my gifts to help people."

You begin to write poetry and you are very successful. You receive praise and gifts from the landowning class. But you take part of this money and help in the education of poor children.

You go down often to visit with the peasants who work the rice paddies. Up the slopes of the hills they labor all day long in hot sun and rain.

You strike up friendships with the peasant children. One bright-eyed little girl catches your attention.

"What are your dreams?" you ask her.

"I do not dream," she tells you. "Not even when I sleep."

You read one of your nature poems to the little girl. It's about a great bird that soars over the marshes to find a beautiful lake beyond the hills.

You tell the little girl she must dream, too. And you provide the money for her to become educated. One of the peasant children you educate becomes a physician and another becomes a teacher.

This gives you as much joy as your poetry.

■ *Turn to page 49.*

You study for several months and then you take the civil service test. You become a member of the *Mandarinate*. Only highly educated and privileged people can join this group. You will be in charge of supervising state projects. You want to use your power to help the people.

When you are not busy, you write poems about the suffering people of China. There are so many of them. In times of famine it is easy to starve. You try to make sure food is shipped to all the provinces when the crops in the country fail.

Some landlords misuse the peasants. This has been going on for a long time. Some poor people have no jobs at all and you must make sure they are given work to do as well as being fed and clothed.

You learn of a poor man whose wife has died. He wants a funeral ceremony for her, but he has no money. You make sure he gets a loan so his wife is properly buried.

Most days you spend trying to protect people from injustice. At night you write poetry. You write about little children working in the rice paddies. You write about brave women who go without food so that their babies can eat.

You gain a reputation as a poet with a big heart.

You have captured the greatness of the ordinary Chinese people in your poetry.

"I was always proud of you," your mother says, "because you were dutiful and honorable. I was proud because you were gifted. But now I am more proud than I ever was, because you have become a very good person. You help those who need help the most."

You live a long and happy life. You do much good, too.

■ *Turn to page 49.*

47

You decide to immediately begin writing poetry. You feel very sorry for the poor farmers in the rice paddies. You try to put your sentiments down. But when you read your poetry to your parents, they frown.

"It sounds very empty and silly," says your mother. "Why don't you write about nature? You can gaze into the sky and see the flights of the grand birds. You can write about that. You have never seen the farmers in the rice paddies. You cannot write what you never saw."

Your father has different advice. "If you want to write about the poor people, you must go where they are. You must meet them and talk to them. Then there will be truth in your poetry," says your father.

"But I have done that. I went to the marketplace and saw a child with her blind mother. My heart ached for the little one when she asked for a pear and her mother had to refuse her," you say.

"Did you speak to the mother?" asks your father. "Did you ask her how she felt? Did you speak to the child?"

"Oh, no," you admit. "You see, father, they were dreadfully dirty. They smelled very bad. I think they must not have bathed in a long time. Even among those fragrant peaches and pears, they offended me." You feel bad at saying such a thing, but it is true.

Your father shrugs. "Perhaps your mother is right. You should be a nature poet after all."

You would rather write about people. So you continue to write sweet, sad verses about poor people. But even you can see they are not very good.

You travel for a while trying to get ideas. But it does not help much. Your poems never have the sound of truth to them. They sound like somebody writing from the outside looking in.

You are always disappointed and sad because your poetic gifts come to nothing.

■ *Turn to page 49.*

The Oldest Printed Book in the World

The world's oldest printed book is the Chinese *Diamond Sutra,* a religious book. In order to print this book, letters or images were carved on blocks of wood. Then ink was put on the blocks. Mulberry bark paper was laid on the inked blocks and the back of the paper was rubbed. Then the words were printed on the front of the paper. This book was printed in A.D. 868. About 200 years later the Chinese used movable clay type, which worked even better

Matching

_____ 1. Subject of the *Diamond Sutra*   a) printing

_____ 2. What Chinese paper was made from   b) religion

_____ 3. This period was the golden age of China   c) T'ang

_____ 4. Modern name for Changan   d) Sian

_____ 5. This was invented first in China   e) mulberry bark

Group Activities

1. Discuss whether you think it is possible to write good poetry or stories about something you know little about. Could the young poet write of poor people without knowing them?

2. Read aloud some of the poems of Li Po and Po Chu-i, famous poets of the T'ang period. Discuss the poems.

3. Using a large atlas, such as *Britannica World Atlas,* find the following cities or historic sites in China:

   Peking   Hwang Ho (yellow river)   Changan (Sian)
   Canton   Yangtze River   Great Wall of China

Individual Activities

1. Find a sample of Chinese writing and write some common words like *man, sun, moon,* and *tree* in Chinese script.

2. Write a short poem about anything.

3. Find out who rules China today. Write the name of the leader, type of government, and the official name of the country in Chinese. This information is in any current almanac.

Life in an English Castle—A.D. 950

You live in an English castle. Your father is a feudal lord. Your castle is called a motte castle. It is in two parts. First you have a big round hill called a motte. On the motte is a wooden tower where you watch the country-side for signs of trouble. Down below at the bottom of the hill is a fenced-in yard called a bailey. That's the second part of the castle. Your home is in the bailey. Your home is called the Great Hall. You also have a horse stable, barracks for soldiers who help protect you, and a garden in the bailey.

The Great Hall where you live has a store-room, kitchen, and bedrooms upstairs.

Right now you are in the wooden tower watching. It is 40 feet tall and very cold and drafty. You hate standing watch, but some-body must always be watching. Otherwise enemies could sneak up and attack the castle. If you see danger, you will sound the alarm and the soldiers will fight off the attackers. You are a youngster, which makes your eye-sight extra sharp.

Suddenly you see a stranger coming. He is on foot and he wears a rough fur coat and sturdy walking boots. He wears a widebrimmed hat and he carries a stick over his shoulder with a bag tied to the end.

You run down the wooden stairs to alert your father. "Stranger coming," you shout breathlessly.

Your father watches the stranger approach. There's a moat (manmade river) around your motte and bailey. A bridge crosses it to let people in. You must open a large wooden gate to allow anyone to enter.

"I have not seen the fellow before," says your father. "I do not know if he means me well or ill." Your father looks at you and asks "Does he look like an honest wayfarer [tra-veler] or a robber?"

■ *If you say a wayfarer, turn to page 53.*

■ *If you say a robber, turn to page 54.*

Find out what your fate is!

"I am sure he is a wayfarer," you say. "He would not come so boldly in midday if he meant us harm."

"Well said," your father agrees. "He is probably a harmless pilgrim."

You open the gate and the man enters.

"Greetings," you call out. "Are you on your way to a holy place?"

The man nods. "I have been to the Shrine of Saint James de Compostella of Spain. I am weary now. If you could spare a bit of bread and wine, I would be thankful. I am going to another shrine then," he says.

You invite the man into your great hall. He sits on a wooden bench and eats bread and cured meat. The man has a bushy beard and a kindly face. You are very curious about him.

"Have you always been a pilgrim?" you ask.

"Oh no. I was once a nobleman with great lands. I left my lands in the care of a steward. Once I wore fine clothes. I wore jewelry. But then I began to think of eternity. What happens after a man lives his short life on this earth? I am not a young man. See my graying hair? My father and mother died before they were as old as I am. I am forty-three," says the man.

Your father looks upset. He is forty!

The pilgrim continues, "I need to go on a pilgrimage to find out why I am on earth. What am I to do with my life before I die?"

When the pilgrim goes his way, your father seems deep in thought. Finally he looks at you and says, "Perhaps that man is right. Your mother died when she was only thirty-five. I am already forty. I spend all my time taking care of the land. I should be having important thoughts like that pilgrim. Perhaps I should put the castle under my steward and go on a pilgrimage, too. Would you go with me?"

It sounds interesting to you, but dangerous, too. Perhaps you should stay here at the castle and help the steward. You could learn much from him.

■ *If you go on the pilgrimage, turn to page 55.*

■ *If not, turn to page 56.*

"I do not like the looks of him," you tell your father. "He is dressed as a pilgrim but once he gets inside he may rob us."

"To be cautious is a virtue," your father says.

"Good folks," cries the man, "I am a hungry pilgrim in need of a little bread."

You ignore him and soon he goes away. Your father turns to you and says, "You gave me wise advice. Follow it yourself. To be generous is good, but to be clever is necessary. Many good persons have lost their lives and property to scoundrels disguised as decent men."

Later in the day you see another stranger coming near the castle. This man looks much different. He is richly clad and well fed. Traveling with him is a bodyguard and a servant pulling a covered cart.

"Ah," says your father, "that man is a cloth trader. The covered cart is loaded with fine linen. I am sure he has goods in there we are in need of."

"But wait." you say, "What if he just looks like a cloth trader? He could be a thief who has killed the real cloth trader, and now he comes with two other robbers to do us harm. He could have swords hidden in the cart."

Your father smiles. "Do not be cautious to a fault, youngster. I have lived long enough to know such a chubby, cheerful face does not conceal the heart of a thief," he says.

You are not so sure. You do not see the man as harmless. You especially do not like the looks of the other two. But are you being too suspicious?

"If you have serious misgivings," says your father, "then we shall bar the gate to these men."

■ *If you urge opening the gate, turn to page 57.*

■ *If not, turn to page 58.*

You and your father put on warm, comfortable clothing. You carry enough bread and cured meat for a long journey. The steward promises to take excellent care of everything in your absence.

You are excited about the trip ahead. You want to see as much of the world as you can.

As you hurry down the road toward nightfall, you see a troubadour coming in the opposite direction. He wears colorful clothing. His shirt, trousers, and cloak are red, green, and gold. He looks as poor as you do, but much more brightly clad! He carries a bedroll, blanket, a few days worth of food, and a lute (a stringed musical instrument like a guitar).

"I shall sleep in yonder meadow," says the troubadour. "Join me, wayfarers."

You happily agree. You sit down in the meadow and exchange stories. The troubadour says, "I am only trying to bring happiness. That is the purpose of my life. I leave people gladder when I leave than they were when I arrived, for their hearts are full of music."

"That is not a bad purpose to have in life," says your father.

"What is your purpose?" the troubadour asks your father.

"I am a noble. I keep a castle. I help defend the whole area. If a nearby village is attacked, the people can take refuge at my castle. My soldiers will defend them."

"That is worthwhile indeed," says the troubadour.

After a long journey, you reach the shrine. You pray there and then head home. You wonder if your father has learned anything from this hard journey.

When you are home, you notice your father is more generous to beggars. He is kinder to you, too. When you talk to him, he really listens. He didn't listen much before. Your father was always a good man, but now he's even nicer!

■ *Turn to page 59.*

You decide not to go on the pilgrimage. You are almost grown and you assure your father he leaves the castle in good hands. The steward is trustworthy and you will be at his side.

The following month after your father is gone, your castle is attacked by a lesser lord who has a grudge against your father. As soon as the enemy knights ride toward your castle, you knock down the bridge. This will make it harder for the enemies to get to the castle. They cannot cross the moat, but they shoot a hail of arrows at you.

Your steward fights valiantly. The knights and soldiers help drive off the enemy. But the steward has taken a severe shoulder wound. You must race across the countryside to an old woman who is a herbalist. Only her healing herbs can save the steward.

You find the old woman's cottage and pound on the door. "Good woman," you cry, "our faithful steward lies dying. Have you strong healing herbs for me?"

The woman gives you agrimony, an herb with yellow flowers. She says, "Boil this in wine, then clean the wound. Use these roots as a poultice. You know how to make a poultice, don't you, young one?"

You nod. You have helped your mother put soft dressings on wounds before.

You thank the woman and hurry home. You follow the old woman's instructions carefully.

In a few days the steward's wound seems better. The wound is not infected and it has begun to knit together.

"I almost died, but your skill and courage saved me," says the steward.

You are proud of how you have grown in your father's absence. When he left, he said goodbye to a child. But when he comes home he will greet an adult.

■ *Turn to page 59.*

You decide your father is right, and you both open the gate to let the men enter with their cart.

"I would guess that you have fine cloth to show me," says your father. "We have need of cotton and linen."

At that moment, the three men draw swords from the cart. They are ruffians! The leader grabs you and another holds a sword tip to your throat! "Listen, nobleman," he shouts at your father, "do not call the soldiers from the barracks or your child will perish quickly. Go yourself to the Great Hall and bring all the gold and jewelry you have, or your offspring will die this day!"

Your father turns white with terror. He hurries off to do as he was told. He fills a chest with many coins and jewels, bringing it back quickly. One of the ruffians loads it into the cart.

"Now release the youngster," your father demands.

"Not so quickly, nobleman. You will then call down your soldiers. We shall take the youngster with us and when we are safely away, you shall see this young one freed," says the leader of the wicked trio.

You are bound hand and foot and tossed into the cart. Then the cart rattles back over the bridge and down the dusty road.

Farther and farther you go until at last the ruffians stop. You are freed and tossed into the dusty road to the laughter of the robbers. The leader says, "When you return to the castle, thank the nobleman for us, youngster, for all the jewels and coin!" He laughs again as you run towards home.

You do not reach the castle until dark, but your father is waiting. Tears of joy run down his face.

"How much treasure did they steal, father?" you ask sadly.

"My only treasure has been returned to me," your father replies, embracing you.

■ *Turn to page 59.*

"I say to bar the gate, Father," you say.

Your father shouts at the three men, "We have no need of cloth today."

"Oh please, nobleman," the chubby man shouts, "at least look at what we have to offer."

Just then you see a sword glittering under the cart cover! Your father draws his own sword and shouts to the soldiers. They swarm from their barracks.

The scoundrels try to escape, but your soldiers capture them. You find they have robbed from many other noblemen and the stolen goods are in the cart.

You take the three men to the dungeon. This is a dark, underground prison with thick walls and no windows. It is below the ground floor of the tower. It's an awful place. You don't remember anybody ever being down there before, except some rats.

You notice that one of the robbers is not much older than you are. You feel bad about that. You think somebody must have led him into a life of crime.

You return to the Great Hall and wait for the sheriff to come and take the ruffians away. You are glad when that happens. It makes you feel funny to think of men in the dungeon under the tower.

Your father takes you aside then. "You were a better judge of character than I. You had misgivings and I did not. I foolishly believed well-clad men are more worthy of trust than poorly clad men."

You enjoy a meal of broiled venison and vegetables. You are warmed by the praise from your father's lips. But you are troubled by the memory of the youngest of the three robbers. "Father, what will become of that young fellow?"

"Ah, he is a hardened thief like the others. He will suffer the penalty deserved by such as he. He will lose his hand," says your father.

Now you really feel sick.

■ *Turn to page 59.*

The Stone Castles

The great stone castles were built later than the motte and bailey castles. One castle built in 1100 had round towers rising 90 feet into the air. The great hall where the lord lived had a huge circular table on the first floor. Upstairs the bedrooms had magnificent beds and lavish furniture. The ceiling of one bedroom was painted blue to look like the sky, with many golden stars sprinkled around.

But even these beautiful stone castles were not pleasant to live in. They were cold and damp. There was just no effective way to heat the rooms in those days. So the rich noble and his family shivered with the cold in the wintertime, unless they sat by the big downstairs fires.

True/False

_____ 1. A motte is a hill.

_____ 2. The castle yard was called a bailey.

_____ 3. Stone castles were built earlier than the motte and bailey castles.

_____ 4. A moat is a waterfall in the mountains.

_____ 5. Stone castles were warm and cozy in the winter.

Group Activities

1. Pilgrimages were supposed to make a person think about important questions in life. Discuss what a person would do today if he or she wanted to spend time thinking about the big questions of life. What are the big questions?

2. When people choose a job today, they want good pay and fulfillment. Discuss what you might want in a job when you are adults. What are the qualities of a good job?

3. Find a picture of a motte and bailey castle. Make drawings or models of them.

Individual Activities

1. In one paragraph, describe what a knight was and what he did in the Middle Ages.

2. Look at a map and find out how far it was for a pilgrim to walk from England or France to the Holy Land (Jerusalem).

3. Draw a coat of arms such as were popular in this era. You will find good samples under Heraldry in the encyclopedia.

Upon the Viking Sea— A.D. 982

ERIK THE RED

You are a Viking youngster. Your ancestors were hated as pirates and robbers. They lived in Sweden, Norway, and Denmark.

"They were sea-going adventurers," your grandfather tells you proudly. "They traveled in Viking ships built of oak planks with high, curved bows. My own father followed Leif and Ingolf to Iceland, and so we are here."

You like Iceland and your coastline home. You help raise sheep and go hunting and fishing. You don't mind the cold weather. You have never lived where the weather is warm.

Now a strong new leader named Eric the Red has arisen among you. But there's a terrible problem. He has been accused of murder. He's an old friend of your father. Your father does not believe the accusation.

"If Eric killed someone, then it was in self-defense," says your father. "It is not fair that they are sending him away from Iceland."

Eric is standing in the midst of his friends. "If you wish to come with me, say so now. We shall all find a new land even better than Iceland," he says.

You would like to go. So would your father. But your mother is worried. She whispers,

"Should we go to a new land with a man accused of murder?"

Your grandfather takes you aside and says, "Youngster, I will be going to England. Many Vikings are settled there. Come with me. It is safer for a youngster in England than in a new settlement with Eric the Red!"

But you like Eric the Red. You know your father will talk your mother into going with him. And Eric the Red describes a new land called Greenland. It sounds good. What should you do? Your mother would prefer you went with your grandfather.

But Greenland sounds thrilling.

■ *If you go to Greenland with your parents and Eric, turn to page 63.*

■ *If you go to England with your grandfather, turn to page 64.*

Find out what your fate is!

You and your parents go with Eric and many other colonists toward Greenland. All of your livestock has been loaded on ships. Your other possessions are on a ship, too. You are leaving Iceland forever. Your heart trembles with the thrill of the unknown.

But as soon as you leave Iceland, storms batter your fleet of 25 ships. Some ships go down in the wind and heavy rain. It is heartbreaking to see friends dying in the sea. It's the most terrible sight you have ever seen. You are not ashamed to cry.

Finally you land in Greenland. There are just 14 ships left. More than half the people you left with are dead.

Eric calls the place where you land the Eastern District. The climate is very good. When your family puts in crops, they grow better than they did in Iceland. The livestock does well, too. You watch the grain grow tall and the vegetables grow large. But you live mostly on fish and mutton from your sheep.

You grow to be an adult in Greenland. You take a spouse and have a little farm of your own. But you feel restless after a while. Is there a land somewhere that is even better than Greenland?

Leif Ericson, Eric the Red's son, says that there is such a land.

"If we traveled west of here, we would find a land with a better climate and soil," Leif says. "I need 35 brave souls to climb into our dragon boats and see what lies west."

You stare at the boats with the dragon heads on their bows. Should you leave your family in the care of your older brother and take the journey? Then, if the land is good, you can return and take your whole family there.

■ *If you go, turn to page 65.*

■ *If you remain in Greenland, turn to page 66.*

You sail to England with your grandfather in a Viking boat with one sail and oars.

Your grandfather builds a house in the countryside with wattle and daub walls, tree logs plastered with mud. You have an open fire in the center of the house to keep warm and cook. You sit on low wooden benches and eat from a long timber table.

You help your grandfather raise sheep and chickens. You find the weather is so much warmer than in Iceland. You can raise many more vegetables and even fruit.

The sad news comes quickly that your parents were lost in a storm off Iceland during the journey. You wonder if you should have gone with them. Maybe you could have helped during the storm. Your grandfather tells you that such thoughts are foolish.

You grow up in England and take a spouse. But then trouble breaks out between your English neighbors and you. You live in an area called the Danelaw. Only Vikings live here. If you try to move to another part of England, there will be fighting.

"The English hate us," a Viking neighbor tells you. "They resent us because we are different."

You know that the English pay large sums of money to some Vikings to get them to go home.

Your neighbor continues in a grim voice. "I am afraid someday the English will try to drive us all out. Maybe we will be murdered."

You are worried, too. You have a family now. Your cousin is moving to Scotland. There are nice hills and lakes there. The soil is good for farming and for raising sheep. Maybe you should go, too.

But you have a nice farm in the Danelaw. You hate to leave all you have worked for.

■ *If you remain in the Danelaw, turn to page 67.*

■ *If you go to Scotland, turn to page 68.*

You sail with Leif Ericson on the westward voyage. You work at one of the many oars to move through violent storms in your swift dragon ship. Your red and white sail fills with wind, but you never overturn.

Finally, after a long westward course, you move sharply north. Then you move south along a beautiful green seacoast.

"Look! An island there," cries one of your companions. "How pretty and green, like springtime."

You row in and find wild wheat and grapes growing.

As you scramble ashore in this new place, you cannot help but quickly sample the grapes. Are they as good as they look?

"Ah, what sweet grapes," you shout. Soon you are all plucking them as fast as you can.

"We will settle here for the winter," Leif says.

You work hard building huts for the colder weather just ahead. You draw delicious salmon from the sea and roast the fish over open fires. It's a time of good eating, excitement, and adventure.

Leif Ericson names this land Wineland because of the fine, sweet grapes. Often it is called Vinland.

Wineland is a wonderful place and you live a good few months here. You build nine buildings and even a blacksmith shop. But you miss your family very much. So, after leaving some stone markers, you return to Greenland in the spring.

You never return to Wineland, but others go back. In your Viking legends there will be many stories of this lovely, fruitful land.

Hundreds of years later, most people doubt that there ever was a real place called Wineland. They are sure it was just a fairy tale told by Vikings. Then, in 1963, the remains of your little colony are found in Newfoundland. So Wineland, or Vinland, is really Newfoundland. You left your mark on history.

■ *Turn to page 69.*

You stay in Greenland and raise sheep. One day while you are tending your flock, you see a darker man peering at you from a distance. He is dressed in animal skins. You are frightened. He is not a Viking. Who is he?

You rush home and gather your friends. You tell them about the man. One older Viking says, "We are not the only people in Greenland."

"Who else is here?" you ask.

"I have seen those dark-skinned ones. They run when you come across one. They seem as frightened of us as we are of them," says the older man.

"Ah, that's a silly story like the ones you tell children to frighten them," another neighbor says with a laugh. "There are no dark-skinned people here."

"No," a woman says. "My husband calls them skraellings. Once he met one face-to-face. My husband was so frightened that he killed the man. He thought the skraelling would kill him. Then my husband buried the man. He was sorry for what he had done."

Now you are really frightened. How many of these skraellings are here? "We must be careful," you say. "Perhaps there are many of them."

"Maybe," says an old woman, "they are just like us, only darker. Maybe we could be friends."

Everybody laughs scornfully at that. But you wonder if maybe it's true. The skraelling you saw looked more frightened than threatening.

You do not see another dark-skinned stranger closely. But others report seeing more of them. They are Eskimo hunters who arrived in Greenland about three thousand years before the Vikings came.

Your children's children battle the Eskimo hunters. But then some of your great grandchildren marry into Eskimo families. By 1350 all the people of Greenland look like Eskimos.

■ *Turn to page 69.*

You remain in the Danelaw and hope for peace. But in 1013, the Danish King Swegen tries to take control of all England. You must leave your farm and your sheep as war rages. Soon Swegen dies and his powerful son, Canute, takes over. Canute is a Dane and he now rules over all of England.

"Canute will be a fine king," you say to your spouse.

"Yes, he will bring peace," your spouse agrees.

You are free to farm again. But you went into debt during the wars. Now you must borrow money from a wealthy neighbor. You need money for seed and to buy new tools.

You go deeper and deeper into debt. Eventually you must sell your farm to the landowner. He allows you to continue farming there. But it is no longer your land. Your heart aches at the thought. You have gone from being a proud landowner to a serf. Now you must farm another person's land!

"Was all this land once ours?" asks your youngest child.

"Yes, and it will be again," you promise. But you wonder if that is true. To recover your land you must pay the landowner everything you owe him. And each year you seem to go deeper in debt.

The landlord demands that you raise and harvest his hay before your own. It is very bitter for you. You must even bring him eggs on Easter. You must ask his permission about what you will plant in the spring. Once you looked forward to spring planting. Now you see it as a hard chore.

You are afraid you will always be a serf. You are even more afraid that your children will be serfs, too. And, sadly, that is just what happens. Your children do not escape the life of serfs, nor do their children.

■ *Turn to page 69.*

You move to Scotland with your spouse and children. You find fine farmland along a southern river. You raise a herd of hardy sheep and grow to love the land.

But Scotland is divided into many kingdoms. Wars are always breaking out between the different kingdoms. One summer, Northmen from Norway attack your village. They come in swift, low-slung boats. You are a Viking too, like them, but now you are a farmer. You resent these invaders. You cannot defend the village and many of your sheep are stolen. Your house is robbed, too. You are injured in a desperate attempt to save your few possessions.

Now you lie in your hut with a swollen, angry wound in your leg. Luckily your spouse is very clever. Your spouse gathers the pulp of the bryony root. It's a wild vine with red and black fruit. This is added to oil from cowslip flowers and primroses and St. John's wort flowers.

Your spouse boils the herbs in wine and then applies them to your wound. In a few days the red, angry-looking infection fades. Your wound has begun to heal!

You are laid up for a long time, though. Your spouse and children must work twice as hard to care for the few remaining sheep and your crops.

When you are well, you remain very vigilant (watchful) against further attacks by the swift boats of the Northmen. Luckily they do not raid again near your village and your life is peaceful.

You spend your entire life in Scotland and you are very happy you came here. You think there is no more beautiful spot on earth. Some of your happiest times are spent roaming the highlands with your children and watching deer grazing on soft meadow grass.

■ *Turn to page 69.*

Did the Vikings Discover America?

In 1898, a large stone was found on a Minnesota farm near the town of Kensington. Some scholars believe that the Kensington stone tells, in runic language, of some Vikings who came there in 1362 and fought with the local Indians. Other scholars believe the stone is a prank. If it is real, it contributes to the evidence that the Vikings were the first Europeans to discover America. The Kensington rune stone is on display in a museum in Minnesota.

Matching

_____ 1. Where the Vikings went in 874

_____ 2. He had to flee Iceland after being accused of murder

_____ 3. The town near where the runic stone was found

_____ 4. The state where the runic stone was found

_____ 5. Eric the Red went to this place from Iceland

a) Kensington

b) Minnesota

c) Greenland

d) Iceland

e) Eric the Red

Group Activities

1. Make some Viking boats. They are one of the easiest types of model boat to make. Instructions may be found in encyclopedias.

2. On a large map find the routes of Viking ships. Find Norway, Sweden, Denmark, England, Scotland, Iceland, Greenland, and Newfoundland.

3. Discuss the Vikings and their bad reputation as sea raiders. How were they different from any explorers who arrived in a land already occupied by people (such as the Indians)?

Individual Activities

1. Imagine you are a Viking in Greenland. Describe in one or two paragraphs your reaction to seeing a dark-skinned stranger looking at you from the distance.

2. Use a large dictionary to find out the origin of the following words:

   ship   mast   law   bread

   Write the Viking word these terms are taken from.

3. Draw a Viking boat.

Bazaars of Baghdad— A.D. 1000

You are a young Arab in Baghdad. Your father is a very successful merchant. You love to wander through the colorful bazaars and see the variety of goods. You smell the spices from China. How heavenly is their scent! You touch the smooth silks, the paper, and glittering gold and silver utensils from China, too. Furs, birch bark, horsehides, nuts, and honey come from Europe. Is there anything anyone could want that cannot be found in Baghdad? You don't think so.

What fun it is to mix with bearded Swedes and tall Indians who bring beautiful pottery. You can meet people from all corners of the earth in the noisy, exciting bazaar.

"I would not trade the life of a merchant for any other," says your father with great relish. He would not mind your becoming a merchant, too. But you have always been drawn to the world of learning. Your mother loves books. She has made you love them, too. Seeing her joy in books has made you want to share that joy. Deep in your heart is a secret desire to be a doctor. Arabic doctors are studying diseases and treating them with great success.

Here can be found the brightest doctors of the whole world. Should you become one of them? There are excellent hospitals to work in. How satisfying it would be to be able to understand infection and contagion and ease the suffering of people with pleurisy or measles or smallpox.

Still, there will be many times you cannot help a sick person and you will share the sadness of a family losing a loved one. You must be very strong for this profession. As a merchant you would not have to deal with such problems.

■ *If you become a doctor, turn to page 73.*

■ *If you become a merchant, turn to page 74.*

Find out what your fate is!

You train to become a doctor. The school you attend has gathered all the knowledge of medicine in the world. You study the Greek books on the human body and diseases. You study Persian books about healing plants. You are very interested in the use of drugs to treat diseases. These drugs come from plants.

As you study, a friend says, "If you have a scientific mind, why not become an alchemist?"

"I have always liked the idea of healing people," you say.

"Indeed. A good and honorable goal. But what if you were the alchemist who solved the problem of changing ordinary metal into gold? What if you found this powder they call the 'philosophers' stone'? Think of the good you could accomplish with all this wealth," says your friend.

You smile. You know all about the great Arab alchemist Jabir Ibn-Hayyan. He lived in about A.D. 750, and he started the search for that dry powder that could make gold from metal. Now you say, "I don't know if there is such a thing. So many clever people have searched and found nothing. Why should I be the one to accomplish it?"

"Ah," laughs your friend, "someone will be the one to work the wonder. Why not you? All the world would lie at your feet. You would be rich and famous. And you could give to the poor and erase the misery of poverty from many."

You ponder that idea. Should you give up your dream of healing people to search for the philosophers' stone? It seems quite ridiculous to do such a thing. Then again, what a marvelous discovery it would be. Why, it could change the world and make you the most honored alchemist of all time!

■ *If you continue studying to be a doctor, turn to page 75.*

■ *If you become an alchemist, turn to page 76.*

You cannot leave the excitement of the bazaar. So you forget about the books and learn at your father's side.

You rise early one morning and walk through Baghdad towards the bazaar. You pass the Palace of the Golden Gate and admire the great green dome atop it. There stands the statue of a mounted warrior.

Each street in the bazaar is assigned to dealers in one kind of product. Market inspectors roam around to make sure prices are fair and quality is good. The inspectors even check on cruelty to animals. If you are selling chickens, you must not mistreat them. They must be comfortably kept in roomy cages until they are mercifully killed.

Your father specialized in cambric (fine white linen). He takes you to the bankers' clearing house at Basra in southeast Iraq. He introduces you to the people you will be dealing with. You can tell he is very pleased with your decision to be a merchant.

You do very well as a merchant for several years. Then you grow restless. You would like to travel to some of the places where all these products in the bazaar come from. Before you settle down to raise a family you want to see a bit of the world.

"Where do you wish to go?" your father asks you.

"I have heard that Cairo is a most beautiful city," you say. "I would like to go there, I think."

"What of Andalusia in Spain?" asks your mother. "I saw it once and I shall never forget it."

You have heard others speak of the magnificent, subtropical Andalusia, with its peach and pomegranate orchards.

But Cairo is such an historic city!

■ *If you go to Cairo, turn to page 77.*

■ *If you go to Andalusia, turn to page 78.*

You finish your studies and fulfill your dream of becoming a doctor. Soon you are called to the home of a young family.

"My young son is fearfully ill," says the anxious father.

"He is our only child," cries the mother. She is a beautiful woman with large, dark eyes. You can see she has been crying.

You enter the sick room to find a small child coughing hard. It is a racking cough that shakes the small body. You recall Avicenna's great medical book, *Canon of Medicine.* You recognize the child's symptoms.

"It is pleurisy," you say.

"What can be done?" asks the father.

You have brought many herbal remedies along with you. Now you remove a powder made from the leaves of the lobelia (plant with blue flowers). You instruct the child to swallow the powder when it is dissolved in water.

"This will help," you say in a soothing voice. You learned in school how important it is for the doctor to be kindly and encouraging.

The medicine causes the child to cough up phlegm (mucus in the chest). Soon he is breathing much easier. He quickly falls into a restful sleep which will do him much good, too. You say, "I will return tomorrow to see how the child is doing."

The young parents thank you. You have already done the child some good and they are very grateful.

When you return the next day, the child is much better. The happy parents cannot praise you enough. They pay you well, too. But your big reward comes when the child gives you a wide smile.

You help many people. But there are some you cannot help. This makes you sad, as you knew it would. But it is all part of being a doctor. And you are never sorry you chose this noble profession.

■ *Turn to page 79.*

You almost believe you will be the one to find the philosophers' stone! You gather all the scientific books that have been written on the subject. You study day and night. You light your lamp so you may study until you fall asleep. You become a master of alchemy. You learn how the Egyptian metalworkers made imitation gold by mixing copper with other metals. But you must make *real* gold!

You learn that the powder called the philosophers' stone must be applied to a common metal. First the metal will turn black. Then, as it grows more pure, it will turn white. Then it will turn red. Finally you will have pure gold.

You work for many years with no success. You grow angry and frustrated. You develop such a bad temper that your old friends start to stay away from you. It is no fun looking for something that may not exist!

Finally you give up the whole idea. If you are to avoid madness, you must study something else. So you begin to study logic. You read the books by the ancient Greeks. Perhaps you will teach logic. But you soon lose interest.

You begin reading books on the law. That is more interesting. After a long time you become a lawyer. You make a good salary, but you aren't very happy.

You always think back to your original dream. You wanted to be a doctor. You let someone's foolish advice set you on a different path. You wasted all those years trying to turn metal into gold. What folly!

You have a spouse now and three bright children. You go walking with them and often give them advice. You are not sure how much of your advice they listen to, but you hope they listen to your most heartfelt piece of advice. "Stay true to your own dreams," you say, over and over.

■ *Turn to page 79.*

You finally decide on Cairo. You are thrilled to be off to the great city.

What an amazing city Cairo turns out to be! You see thousands of brick houses. Many of them are five and six stories high. There are thousands of shops, too. You can buy just about anything you want.

At night lamps light the streets. What a wonder. It is like daylight in the darkness of night! Sometimes soldiers riding horses go by, but most of the people ride donkeys. You can hire a donkey on any street corner. You look around until you see a very good-natured-looking donkey and you climb astride. You guessed right. This donkey is easy to control. He will willingly take you all around.

"Look," you say to a new friend who rides a donkey beside you, "the doors of the houses are not even locked. The jeweler just puts a cord across the doorway when he leaves and nobody dares enter."

Your new friend nods. "The punishment for a thief is very harsh. His hands are chopped off very promptly. Very few are bold enough to steal when such a penalty awaits them. That, you see, is the secret to good order. Swift, sure, and terrible punishment," he says.

You travel to the Mosque of Ibn Touloun. You admire the great open court with a fountain in the center. A single minaret (tall slender tower) rises into the bright blue sky. From here the people are called to pray. You walk through the arches in the Mosque. Then you step outside and travel by your donkey to the Al-Azhar University. What a splended center of learning!

As you hurry through a crowd, you feel someone bump into you. You grab for your coins! You have been robbed. You see a young pickpocket running away. You run after the boy and grab him. "Thief! Give me what you have taken!" you shout.

The boy looks terrified. He thinks you will turn him over to the authorities. But you scold him and send him off when you have your coins back. You hope he does not steal again.

You feel good about showing compassion. That too is part of your Islamic belief.

■ *Turn to page 79.*

You travel to Andalusia and it is even more beautiful than you expected. You go to the great Mosque at Cordoba. You walk through a forest of columns supporting arches.

The streets of Andalusia are paved and well lighted by lamps. You visit one of the fine homes and sit on a marble balcony with other young people.

"When the weather cools," says your host, "heat comes out of hot-air ducts under the floors."

You look down at the mosaic floor and say, "What a wonderful convenience."

The house is surrounded by a handsome garden with a clear pool. Fountains and little waterfalls spill over rocky ledges. In the orchards around the house you pick peaches and pomegranates from the trees.

You pluck a golden pomegranate and peel the tough rind. Then you bite into the fruit. The seeds in the flesh burst. Your mouth fills with sweet, tangy juice. The sweet, soft peaches are equally marvelous.

Then you go to see the merchants of rich silk fabrics. Striking red peacocks strut on the fabrics. You must take some of these home and show them to your father. Even in the bazaars of Baghdad you have not seen such gorgeous fabrics.

When you return to Baghdad, you have samples of the special fabric. You show them to your father, who is very excited.

You make arrangements to sell the fabric in Baghdad and make more money than you have ever made. Now you will travel regularly to Andalusia for fabric. It will be a highlight of your year. You never tire of this beautiful city.

Even when you are married, you will travel often to Andalusia, and take your family with you.

■ *Turn to page 79.*

Arab Scientists

Arab scientists discovered the science of optics. Arab chemists discovered basic substances like alum, borax, sodium carbonate, and nitric acid. Arab doctors such as Rhazes and Avicenna made the first scientific description of diseases like smallpox and measles. Avicenna, a Persian physician, was a good example of a golden age of learning in the Arab world. He lived around A.D. 1000 and he wrote in Arabic. Hundreds of years after Avicenna's death, physicians were still using his brilliant articles on medicine.

True/False

_____ 1. Baghdad is in Egypt.

_____ 2. There were fine hospitals in Iraq around A.D. 1000.

_____ 3. Avicenna was a silk merchant in Cairo.

_____ 4. Rhazes was an Arab doctor.

_____ 5. The Arabs did not study the science of optics.

Group Activities

1. Discuss life in the Arab world around A.D. 1000. What did you find surprising? What did you find pleasant or unpleasant about it?

2. On a large map, find the old Islamic empire. Also find, on a modern map, the countries that are primarily Islamic today.

3. Arabesque was a fanciful ornamental pattern, either painted or carved. Find copies of it and make a poster showing Arabesque style (circles, star shapes, and curving lines and ribbons).

Individual Activities

1. Islamic people valued calligraphy (beautiful writing). It was a high form of art. Copy some examples of Islamic calligraphy.

2. Imagine you live in A.D. 1000 and have caught a young pickpocket. Describe in one or two paragraphs why you would or would not turn the pickpocket in.

3. Make a sketch or model of a mosque.

In Robin Hood's Time—1160

You are a youngster in England and your family is very hungry. The only wild game you and your family are allowed to shoot are rabbits and pigeons. You live with your widowed mother and two little sisters at the edge of the royal forest where there are many deer. But only military men and royal barons can hunt in the royal forest. Your mother and oldest sister are quite good with the bow and arrow. But you are best. You must find something for your family.

This year the family wheat and rye crop was very poor. You have even killed and eaten your chickens, so now there are no eggs. Today your young sisters cry with hunger. You must take your bow and arrow and bring home game.

"I will go into the royal forest and shoot a deer. Then there will be plenty of fresh meat for all of us," you say. "We can salt what is left over and have good food for many days."

"Oh, child," groans your mother, "What if the royal forest guards catch you? They will not even have mercy on your youth!"

"I will be very careful," you promise.

As you leave with your bow and arrows, you feel very grown up, but scared too. There is terrible punishment for anyone caught hunting illegally in the royal forest. For the first offense of killing a royal deer the hunter loses arrow fingers. For the second offense there is blinding. For the third offense, the poor hunter is hanged!

Dare you risk it? Should you perhaps look for rabbits and pigeons instead and leave the royal deer alone?

■ *If you hunt for deer, turn to page 83.*

■ *If you hunt for rabbits and pigeons, turn to page 84.*

Find out what your fate is!

You cannot bear the cries of your small sisters anymore. You must head for the royal forest in the light of the early dawn. Deer often graze at this hour. The thought of roasting venison and your family's joy chases your fears.

You pause beside a large forest oak. There are ash, beech, elm, and chestnut trees around the meadow just ahead. And there is a small deer! Just perfect. You shall be able to carry it home. You raise your arm and place an arrow in your bowstring. Your bow arm is straight out. You grip the bow handle lightly. You draw the bow string back until it reaches your jaw.

Then you let the arrow go! Your arrow kills the deer instantly. You scramble forward, your heart pounding with excitement and triumph.

You swiftly tie the animal's hooves together and carry it across your back. As you race for home, the shouts of men fill the forest! The forest guard! Are they on your trail? Did someone see you enter the royal forest and warn them? People are so desperate now that they will betray a neighbor for a few coins.

Your heart pounds in terror as you move. The deer you carry grows heavier on your small shoulders. You stagger under the weight. You look to the marshy thickets to the south. You could hide there, maybe. But that means going out of your way on your journey home.

Perhaps you ought to just keep to the trail, moving as fast as you can. Perhaps the men you hear are not even after you. If you keep on the trail, you shall be home swiftly and out of danger.

You pause for a few seconds, getting your breath. You must decide quickly—run forward or hide in the thicket? The voices of the men grow louder!

■ *If you hide in the thicket, turn to page 85.*

■ *If you keep to the path, turn to page 86.*

You lose your boldness. The punishments are too severe. Instead you hunt for rabbits and pigeons. But you have no luck and must go home empty-handed.

You sit on a bench in the thatched-roof cottage your father built before he died so young. Your feet stir the dust on the dirt floor. You and your poor mother and sisters have only a few half-rotten potatoes left to eat. Because of failed crops, rabbits have become scarce, since so many people hunt them. The rabbits that remain are getting too wily to be caught. Even when you do catch one, the meat is stringy.

Your little sisters cry with hunger again. You must do something. Will you all die as your father did? "I watched father work leather and saw wood," you say. "Maybe if I went to town I could be a helper."

Your mother looks at you and says, "You are only a youngster."

"Many younger than I work," you say. "Ten-year-old boys and girls work. Even younger ones do."

You ask permission of your lord first. You cannot do anything without asking his permission. He makes sure you have done all the chores he wants, and then he gives you permission.

You head for town, hoping to earn a few coins. You look down the narrow streets. An old man runs a saddlery at the corner. You know him. He is a miser. He would work you hard, but at least you could be sure of a few coins at the end of the day.

Farther down the street, men are building a house. It's a large house. Surely they would let you carry tools for the workers. You could clamber up and bring them what they needed. You are very agile. But they are strangers. Maybe they would cheat you at the end of the day.

■ *If you ask for work at the saddlery, turn to page 87.*

■ *If you go to the house, turn to page 88.*

You run toward the thicket, scratching yourself on the thorny bushes as you crouch down. You tremble as the cries of the forest guards draw closer. What if they catch you? You look down at your fingers and a chill goes up your spine.

You crawl deeper into the thicket, dragging the deer after you. You are almost afraid to breathe. You see the hated figures of the guards prowling around in the distance.

And then they move on. Praise God, you whisper. They did not even look in your direction. You crawl from the thicket when they are safely gone. You hurry towards home and soon you reach your thatched hut.

You and your mother skin and cut up the animal. Soon the cottage fills with the wonderful aroma of broiling venison. At last there will be meat for your poor family. Already their eyes shine with anticipation.

"There will really be meat," cries your mother.

"Yes, enough for all," you say proudly. "This night nobody goes to bed hungry."

Your family feasts on the venison and a few boiled potatoes. A rosy glow comes back to the cheeks of your sisters. For the first time in many days there are smiles all around.

You have salted and put away some of the meat. But soon you must hunt again.

One morning you see a wild boar. It is legal to hunt wild boars, but dangerous. Most hunt them on horses. But you are too poor for a horse. You have only a sharp spear. You lunge at the beast, killing him with your spear. You are filled with great joy. With the salted venison and the meat of this wild pig, you will have meat enough for the winter.

You sing as you drag the boar home.

■ *Turn to page 89.*

You continue to run down the trail. But the royal guards are upon you!

"Scoundrel," shouts the chief guard. "You have killed one of the king's deer on royal land."

You bow down low, hoping to touch the cruel man's heart. "Have pity. My father is dead. My poor mother and small sisters depend on me to live. We have only a few rotten potatoes for a family of four."

"Vile youth," snaps the guard, "there is no excuse for breaking the forest law. You lazy serfs would sooner kill all the deer in the forest than work your land properly."

You are bound and taken before the local sheriff.

"Do you deny that you killed the king's deer?" the sheriff asks.

You cannot very well deny it, for you were caught with the deer. "No," you say, "but the starvation of my family drove me to it."

The sheriff sneers at you. "Do you look for pity, young wretch? You well knew the penalty when you killed the king's deer. Even a child of seven knows that, and you are beyond seven by some years!" He turns to the men beside him. "Bring the axe," he says.

"No, no please," you cry.

The man raises the axe over your fingers. Then the sheriff shouts, "Scaring the wretch is good enough. But mind me! Next time you are caught, your youth will do you no good. You shall lose your fingers!"

You trudge toward home without the deer you shot. What will become of your poor family now?

In the days ahead you and your mother trap small game. Your littlest sister dies in the cold, hungry winter. Life is bleak and hopeless. You grow bitter against those who rule England. You wish success to the growing bands of robbers roaming the forest.

■ *Turn to page 89.*

You go to the old man at the saddlery.

"A stripling like you wants work?" he barks.

"Yes, Sir. I will do anything. I need some coins to buy food for my hungry family," you say.

The old man makes leather coats, saddles and shoes, leather armour, and vessels for holding wine. "You have no skills," he says, "but I will let you soften the leather with fats."

You labor all day working oils into the leather hides. You work for twelve long hours. Your back aches and you almost faint from hunger. You have not had a bite to eat all day.

Near dark, the old man says, "I suppose you want your money now."

"Yes, sir, please," you say.

He drops a few coins into your hand and you run to the market to buy food. You have three coins; this will buy four pigeons, two pounds of cheese, and three dozen eggs.

When you arrive home at your small cottage, your mother is overjoyed to see all the food. You have lived only on potatoes for more than a week. Cheese, pigeon meat, and eggs look like a great feast.

"I traded some mending for a little flour," your mother says, "so we have bread as well!"

Now you have bread to go with the food you bought! The pigeon meat does not go far. A few bites and it is gone. But the bread and cheese are filling.

You are glad at last your family has been fed. Tomorrow, early in the morning, you will go hunting again. If you are lucky you will find a boar. They are legal to hunt. But tonight you sleep peacefully. Nobody is tossing with hunger pangs.

■ *Turn to page 89.*

You join the laborers building the house in town. The man in charge is a jolly fellow. You like him at once. He promises you a good wage at the end of the day.

"If you do well, you shall have five coins by sunset," he says.

You can handle the axe, chisel, and saw. You have built sheds and fences. But you are not a specialist. You could make a useful rough wooden bench, but not a chest of drawers to satisfy your lord, or a wagon.

You work on the timber framing of the house. You do not make any big mistakes. You feel you have done a good job at the end of the day. Your back aches, but you look forward to getting the five coins.

"Ah," says the chief carpenter, "your work was not too good. You were much too slow. I can only give you one coin. You did not earn more than that."

You are outraged. "That is unjust! I worked as quickly as the others. One coin is not enough to buy food for my family."

The man looks angry. "Do not cause trouble, serf. I will call the sheriff and have you flogged for threatening me if you aren't careful. Now take the coin you have earned and be glad of it!"

You have no choice. You take the coin and go to the market. You had hoped to buy a little meat, but the cheapest meat costs more than you have. All you can buy is a two-pound cheese.

You head home sadly. You are ashamed to face your mother with only a cheese! But when you reach home, your mother has good news. "I have gotten flour and baked a loaf of bread. The cheese and the bread will fill us up nicely," she says.

Tomorrow you will try to hunt again. But tonight there is bread and cheese and you are grateful.

■ *Turn to page 89.*

Robin Hood

The legends of Robin Hood, his friend Maid Marian, and the band of merry men come from this period in England. Nobody is sure if he lived or not. But people like him did live. They were honest people, angry at the injustice of the government.

Robin Hood was said to live in Sherwood Forest. He robbed the wicked, greedy lords and helped the poor. He hunted the king's deer and laughed at the verderers who couldn't catch him. If Robin Hood did live, he may have been the Earl of Huntingdon, and he may be buried in Yorkshire, England.

Matching

_____ 1. Serfs could not hunt these in the royal forest.

_____ 2. The punishment for a first offense of hunting in the royal forest was loss of

_____ 3. Where Robin Hood lived

_____ 4. Who Robin Hood may have been

_____ 5. A royal forest guard

a) Earl of Huntingdon

b) verderer

c) fingers

d) deer

e) Sherwood Forest

Group Activities

1. The harsh forest laws were written to save the wildlife in the forest. Discuss whether they were fair or unfair. Why?

2. Discuss the life of a serf in England at this time. Was it harder or easier than a poor person's life today in your city or town?

3. Make posters or models of large stone castles.

Individual Activities

1. In one paragraph each, describe what two of these people did for a living:

   a) verderer   b) saddler   c) serf

2. Look up and read a story about Robin Hood.

3. In one or two paragraphs, explain how the reason for hunting today in this country differs from the reason for hunting in England in 1100.

A Life of Service— 1180

You are a young Italian. You have not given too much thought to what you will do in life. Your thirteen-year-old cousin joins a monastery. Now you wonder what sort of life you want.

This morning, in church in Naples, you listen attentively to the priest's sermon. He is telling the story of Dives and Lazarus from the Bible. Dives was a rich man who would not help Lazarus the beggar. When Dives died, he fell into hell. You shudder at the story.

You go home with your parents to your beautiful villa in Naples. Your house is made of wood and stone. You have plenty of good food. But there are many people with no homes and little food. They are so poor they live on the streets and beg. You think they are like Lazarus.

"Sometimes I feel very sorry for the poor," you tell your father. "I feel sad seeing them suffer."

"Nonsense, child," your father mutters. "They are lazy. They are a big nuisance standing around. I must get to my business and they are in my way. I wish a wind would blow them all into the sea."

You feel terrible to hear such talk. For the next few months you think a lot about your future. You are at the age when young people make important choices. You decide to join a religious order as your cousin did. You want to care for the sick and poor. Your parents will be angry, but you must follow your heart.

But some religious orders have grown lazy and useless. You don't want to join one of them. Maybe you should take your small savings and start your own group. You are young, but you are full of great ideas.

■ *If you join a religious order, turn to page 93.*

■ *If you try to start your own, turn to page 94.*

Find out what your fate is!

A friend has told you about a religious order in a small village near your home. You decide to go there and join. You dread telling your father, but one day you tell him, firmly and simply.

"I must give my life to this work," you say.

"Are you mad?" screams your father. "I will lock you away before I let you do such a thing!"

You pretend that your father has frightened you into changing your mind. Then, one day you pack all your belongings and hurry away from the villa in Naples. You walk down the road with tears in your eyes. You love your family and you hate to leave them. But you are grown up and you must follow your heart.

You walk all morning until you come to a steep hill. At the top of the hill is a group of stone buildings behind some trees. That is the place you seek.

You have heard that life is very strict here. You must pray at midnight and early in the morning. For your first meal of the day you will eat only a few ounces of bread or porridge and drink watery wine. At the other meals you will have simple bread and cheese. All day long you must find the sick and homeless and help them. This is the life you want. You do not want comfort and ease. You want to serve God and suffering humanity.

When you arrive at the priory (the religious house) you meet the prior (head). The prior has nice ruddy cheeks and a warm welcome for you. "Come to the parlor," you are asked.

You find a lovely parlor with nice drapes and carved chairs. You are served a snack of thick meat, buttered bread, and sweet little green peas. The dormitory has nice fluffy beds. It is all too rich for you!

"Will I work with the sick?" you ask.

"Oh no," says the prior. "We are a hotel for travelers. No sick people here."

This is all wrong for you! But perhaps if you joined this order you could change it into something better. You could turn the members' attention to the poor.

■ *If you decide not to join, turn to page 95.*

■ *If you join, turn to page 96.*

You decide to start something on your own. You take the small sum your parents gave you for the time when you decided to be married. This is yours and you have a right to it. You pack a few pieces of clothing and some bread and cheese in a sack, and you leave your parents' villa. From now on you will serve God and your fellow human beings.

You head down a street where you have often seen poor beggars. Now you find a poor man lying in the street.

"Come, my friend," you say, "I have some bread and cheese for you."

The man looks up, and you see his face is terribly disfigured. His skin is white and wasted. He has leprosy. You are shocked and sickened by the sight. You are afraid if you go any closer to him you will catch the disease, too. You start to turn away.

Then you stop yourself. No! You have decided to give your life to help the most abandoned people. Nobody is more abandoned than the poor lepers. You reach down and touch the man's bent shoulders. "Here, brother, here is some food," you say.

The fellow takes the bread and cheese and eats hungrily. "Where do you live?" you ask gently.

"Here," the man says, pointing to the street.

"You must have a shelter," you say. "I will look for a place for you."

You hurry to find some young friends of yours in Naples. You know they are goodhearted. They want to help the poor and needy.

"I must find a place where poor lepers can live," you tell your friends.

"Lepers?" they gasp in one voice. Soon they are scurrying away!

Maybe doing things on your own is not the way to go. Perhaps you ought to find a religious order to join after all. Or could you make a home for poor lepers on your own?

■ *If you go on alone, turn to page 97.*

■ *If you join a religious order, turn to page 98.*

You shake your head, thank the prior, and hurry away. This place is not for you.

"But wait," shouts the prior. "Why, many nobles stop here on their travels. You will find it very pleasant."

"I can see it is pleasant," you say. "But that is not what I want."

"Silly goose," mutters the prior as you flee.

You walk through many villages until you come to a large almshouse beside a chapel. The dormitory here is simple. Curtains separate the plain, hard beds from each other.

Out in the garden you find nice vegetables, and the orchard is full of apples and pears. There are pigs and goats and chickens. A pond provides a home for ducks who lay big eggs in the meadow grass.

"Our work is the care and teaching of orphan children," says the prior of this house.

"Oh, that sounds like a wonderful task," you say. You join the religious order. You don't mind sleeping at night on a mattress filled with straw. You didn't come here for cushions and comfort.

When the orphan children are picked up off the streets, they are sad and ragged. Their fathers have died in the many wars that are always going on. Their mothers have died of poverty and disease. Now the little ones are alone.

You take the children down to see the ducks, and that usually brings a smile to their faces. (Who can look at a duck and not smile a little?) Then you give the children clean clothes and a nice meal of hot bread and grape jelly with raisin pudding. Only when they feel comfortable here do you begin to teach them.

You love this work more each year. You have cared for hundreds of children by the time you are old. You are well satisfied with the life you have chosen.

■ *Turn to page 99.*

You decide to stay at the priory and change it into something better.

Many travelers come to stay here. Many are nobles who want to hunt in the nearby woods. Others are wealthy merchants on their way across Italy.

You provide nice rooms for your wealthy guests. Rugs hang over the windows. The mattresses are soft and plump and candles offer light. The meals are more delicious than you had at home.

One day a poor man asks to stay at the priory. "I have a penny," he says, "and I can give you that. I was told this would be enough since I have no more."

"Sorry, dear fellow," says the prior with a cheery smile, "the charge is ten pennies, and many of our guests pay more."

The poor man walks on. You feel sort of sad. But you have grown to like this place. You love the venison that the hunters bring and share with you. You have never tasted such tender and flavorful venison. And you have the most delicious apple and cherry pies with fresh, thick cream on top. Why, you are getting a bit chubby yourself after so much good living!

When you first came here, there were prayers at midnight, but not anymore. The prior says you all need your rest. You like to sleep late. You don't do much of anything except sometimes change the bedding for the guests.

One day when you are middle-aged, you wonder sadly what has happened to your beautiful dream of serving others. Little by little you lost it! You let this comfortable life take it from you. You ponder this for a while, but then you smell venison roasting and you forget everything and rush to the kitchen.

■ *Turn to page 99.*

You walk the streets alone until you find an old house in a woods at the edge of town. You enter and find it filthy and abandoned. A big rat runs across your shoe and you stifle a scream.

But the place can be cleaned up and you can rent it for a few pennies a month. You immediately begin to sweep and mop until the house is very clean. Then you patch the holes in the roof. As you work, another young Italian comes along.

"What are you doing?" asks the stranger.

"I am fixing this house up for the poor lepers who have nowhere to go," you say.

"I will help you," says the stranger.

The work goes twice as fast now. Between the two of you, you make the house livable. Then you find the poor leper you saw before and you bring him here.

"There is only straw to sleep on," you say, "but it is clean straw."

The leper is very thankful. He smiles at you and his face does not seem so awful. You are used to it now and it does not bother you so much.

In a month you have five lepers living at this house. Your new friend helps you every day. Other people donate furniture and food. For the first time since they got sick, the lepers have somebody to care for them and give them friendship.

You have started a new religious order. Soon others join you, and you build a self-supporting village for lepers. They have vegetable gardens and orchards and cows and sheep.

Your fame spreads far and wide, but you really don't care. You love the lepers you care for and they love you. It is said that you are a saint, but you laugh and say you don't feel like a saint. You just feel like getting outside and showing the sunset to a little child who has leprosy and must be made to smile.

■ *Turn to page 99.*

You are afraid you are just not the kind of person who can start things on your own. So you find a priory many miles south of your home. It's a very big building with a large infirmary to care for the sick. It is clean and orderly. There is a row of low beds on both sides of a big room. On a table there are many bandages and herbs to make medicines.

You join the religious order that runs this place. You begin caring for the sick and you enjoy the work. But you soon realize that you are alone most of the time. Where are the others who belong to this order? Perhaps they are praying, you think.

You go to the chapel where you pray each morning at dawn. It's a nice little chapel filled with beautiful religious art. But it is empty! Your friends are not here.

"Where are they?" you ask aloud. You search in the kitchen. Why, there are loaves of bread sitting there waiting to be baked. There are grapes to be pressed into wine! But no people.

Finally you go to the warming room. This is a room with large stoves. It is the only specially heated room in the priory. The members of the religious order go there to warm up for a few minutes after a cold job, like going outside to gather eggs or firewood. The walls are lined with seats.

Oh-oh! Here you find all the missing people! They are sitting here talking and getting warm. When they see you, they hurry back to their duties. You don't say a word because you are new here. You can't be scolding these people who are older than you. But something about your idealistic young face stirs their hearts.

Slowly, your presence changes the priory into a better place. Everybody seems to be more enthusiastic. You have been like a light shining in the gloom. You are very glad you came.

■ *Turn to page 99.*

Francis of Assisi, Italy

One of the most famous founders of a religous order was Francis of Assisi. The fun-loving son of a wealthy family, he gave up everything to serve the poor. His love for the whole world even included animals. He started the custom of spreading crumbs to feed wild birds. (They are still fed in the marketplace of Assisi.) It all began when Francis held out the hand of friendship to a dying leper. He began by loving the most abandoned people. He ended up by loving all.

Matching

_____ 1. Rich man in the Bible story   a) Assisi

_____ 2. Poor man in the Bible story   b) Italy

_____ 3. The city where Francis lived   c) Dives

_____ 4. Francis started the custom of feeding wild   d) Lazarus

_____ 5. The country where Assisi is located   e) birds

Group Activities

1. Idealism is wanting to give your life for a great cause. Discuss who the idealists in the world today are.

2. What can ordinary people do to make the world better? Find at least ten things anybody can do.

3. Discuss ways you could help to make your country better. If you could make one change, what would it be?

Individual Activities

1. Choose one of the following people and write a paragraph about him or her.

   a) Benedict of Nursia   b) Saint Clare

2. In your opinion, who is the most idealistic person in the world today? Explain your choice in one paragraph.

3. Name one thing you would like to do this year that would be called idealistic. It can be a small thing. Explain in one paragraph.

Sunday in London— 1190

It's a pleasant Sunday afternoon in London. You are a student home on vacation. At school you attended many lectures and took a lot of quizzes. Now you need a rest!

"I had to get up at five o'clock every morning," you complain to your parents. "We went to the chapel to pray. Then for the next seven hours we heard lectures. After all that, we had to do still more. For the rest of the day we had to memorize what we wrote down from the lectures."

Your mother smiles and says, "Why there must be some time for recreation."

"For two hours after lunch we got a little bit of recreation time. Usually I'd be so tired I'd just go to bed. But sometimes I would talk to my friends. I'm just so glad to be home. Now at last I can do something I enjoy. Vacation is wonderful!" you say.

"Well, what will you do on this fine day?" your father asks.

"My friend is coming over with all kinds of good suggestions," you answer. And, sure enough, your friend is arriving now.

"Are you ready to go to the boar fights?" asks your friend.

"The boar fights?" you gasp. "That sounds awful."

"I know, but neither of us have ever been to a boar fight. Wouldn't you like to see what it's like?" asks your friend.

"How about going to the horse exhibition instead? I love to see beautiful horses," you say.

"All our friends are going to the boar fights. Are you afraid of something you have never done before? Why everybody has seen them once," says your friend. "I can't believe you are afraid of a little violence!"

You feel your face turn red. Maybe you should see the boar fights, *just once.*

■ *If you go to the boar fights, turn to page 103.*

■ *If you go to the horse exhibition, turn to 104.*

Find out what your fate is!

"Well, I suppose I could just take a look," you say. "But if I don't like it, I'll leave right away."

You and your friend walk to a field where a large crowd has gathered. You recognize some of your friends from college. You don't feel so strange now. It does seem that everybody is here—men, women, even children. Everyone is in a happy holiday mood.

Suddenly you see the center of all the attention. There are large, angry looking boars in cages. They have large tusks like elephants. They are in a high state of excitement.

"Look, they are anxious to fight," says a woman. "Those are really fighters today. It will be a good contest. Sometimes they bring cowardly boars."

You hear savage barking. You turn to see big, wild-looking dogs on leashes. The men can hardly hold the dogs. Saliva runs from their open, red jaws.

"This is going to be something," a man says. "The dogs and the boars are good competitors."

You feel very funny. You wish you had not come. But you are hemmed in by the crowd (and you are too embarrassed to leave now!).

The boars are freed from their cages and the dogs set on them at once. It is a horrible, bloody sight. The tusks of the maddened boars slash at the snarling dogs. You see one dog ripped badly in the stomach. He lies moaning and bleeding.

"I hate this!" you shout. You turn and push through the crowd.

Your friend runs after you. "What's wrong?"

"It was ugly and awful and I hated it," you snap. You rush on alone, walking along the river bank where the public cook shops are. The air is fragrant with roasting fish and fresh bread. You buy some bread and fish and make a meal of it. Now you must do something else to forget the ugly scenes of the boar fight.

There's a ball game nearby. That should be fun to watch. Or just a simple woodland walk might relax you.

■ *If you go to the ball game, turn to page 105.*

■ *If you take the woodland walk, turn to page 106.*

You insist on going to the horse exhibition. You are not going to watch dogs and boars fight!

When you arrive at the field where the exhibition is held, you see many important people. Earls and barons and knights gather to see the finest horses in London. And what a sight it is!

"Look at those high-stepping palfreys," you say. "Their coats gleam like satin!"

"Yes," your friend says. "They are saddle horses trained for the road. Some are trained just to carry women on side saddles."

"Oh, don't you love those colts," you cry. "They are young and restless, like us!"

You walk over to the big sumpter packhorses. "Look at their big muscles. No wonder they can carry such heavy loads," your friend says.

"Here come the war-horses!" somebody shouts. You all make way as the war-horses march along. They are very expensive. Their ears are trembling with excitement. These are the horses who will carry brave knights into battle. You feel sorry for them. You feel sad for the young knights, too.

You wander over to another part of the field where country people are selling swine and cattle and woolly white sheep. They are also selling plough horses. You draw close to a long-legged foal (young horse) who dances away in the meadow after a butterfly.

You are delighted by the sight of the horses. As a small child you often rode horses at your uncle's manor in the country.

A strange thought comes to you. You are going to the university to prepare for a career in teaching literature. You love books, but you love the out-of-doors, too. Maybe you should spend a year at your uncle's manor. He is getting on in years, and you could help him with the business end of his manor. It would be such fun to ride horses again. But if you interrupt your university studies, will you ever get back to them?

■ *If you go back to the university, turn to page 107.*

■ *If you go to your uncle's manor, turn to page 108.*

You go to a large field where a group of boys is playing ball. The students of each school have their own ball. The fathers of the boys stand on the sidelines cheering their sons on. The fathers seem more excited than the boys. They seem more upset when their sons lose than the boys do, too.

You watch for a while and then wander around to meet other young people. They are running, jumping, and wrestling. One young student is practicing hurling a javelin.

"I can throw farther than that," you say to the student.

"Well come on and try," says the javelin thrower.

Grasping a slim spear, you start running. This is fun. You and your brothers used to throw javelins just in play when you were younger. It was fun to see who could throw it farther. You hurl the spear and it makes a great arc. Then it digs into the earth a few inches behind the javelin thrower's mark.

"Ha, I win," says your new friend.

"Well, I'm out of practice. Let's do it again. I can do better than my first try," you say.

Your friend throws the javelin again and the mark is still farther.

Once again you grasp the javelin and run to the line, letting the spear go. To your delight, your mark is the best anybody has made all afternoon.

You hear a round of cheers and you glow with pride. You have lunch with some new friends and you are relaxed and happy as you head for home.

And then you hear a dog bark. You wince. You remember the poor dog slashed by the boar. You hope he isn't suffering anymore. You are so sorry you went to the boar fight. You are afraid you will always remember the ugliness of it. It is in your brain now and not even a happy afternoon with friends can wipe it away.

■ *Turn to page 109.*

You walk into the woodland toward a stream that races over smooth stones. What a nice sound it makes. How peaceful.

You hear mill wheels turning in the distance. You go deeper into the woodland. Birds sing from the trees. You cannot imagine that just a few hours ago you saw that awful boar fight! What cruelty! Will you ever be able to forget it?

You keep on walking until you see a red deer in a glade just ahead. It's a stag with great antlers. When it sees you it sprints gracefully away.

You think you should be turning around and heading back now. But just as you do, you see a creature with dark grey bristles and long snout. Alongside the animal are her young. They are small and striped yellow and dark brown. It's a wild boar, just like the ones you saw at that boar fight.

You don't want to alarm the boar. She might attack you if she thought you were a threat to her young. You very carefully walk away in another direction. You don't run or leap or do anything that would startle her.

You glance back to see that the boar is not following you. She would rather take care of her babies and eat bugs and worms than tangle with a human being like you.

When you look again, the boar is gone.

You hurry from the woodland then, your mind filled with all the wonderful sights you have seen. You wonder what London will be like for your children and grandchildren. Will there always be woodland near the city for people to roam in on a Sunday afternoon? You hope so.

You hope there are no more boar fights then. You will gather many of your friends together one day soon and work for a law against boar fighting. Maybe you will not be successful right away. But someday this cruel, bloody sport will be illegal. You are sure of it.

■ *Turn to page 109.*

         Choosing Your Way Through the World's Medieval Past

You decide you cannot risk interrupting your education. When your vacation is over, you head back to school.

Your favorite lecturer has become ill and a new professor is now lecturing in his place. What a disappointment. He is supposed to be teaching the subject of logic, but you cannot understand a word he says. You and your fellow students decide not to attend his lectures. If students do not attend lectures, the professor does not get paid and he must leave. Your strategy works and you get a much better professor.

You study hard and pass your examination in literature. You become a lecturer the next fall.

There are strict rules governing the life of a professor. You must begin lecturing just after the bell rings. You must stop lecturing within one minute after the last bell. You are not allowed to be absent without permission from the head of the department.

You are very nervous as you begin your career. What if the students don't like you? You must get at least five students to attend each lecture or money is deducted from your pay. And the pay is low enough anyway!

You begin your lectures on a cold, rainy morning. You try to speak in a strong, clear voice. The students have no books, but you have a big thick book. Each and every page of the book must be covered.

"You are talking too fast," says a student.

You speak more slowly and then another student says, "You speak so slowly that I am falling asleep."

Your students are very lazy. They don't like to write much. Any when you give a quiz, they say it was unfair. You did not grade them justly.

One day when you come to class, there are no students. You see them out on the grass staring at you. They know how to get rid of a teacher they don't like. And they get rid of you.

You hope you get another class and do better with it.

■ *Turn to page 109.*

You head for the countryside and your uncle's manor. You ride in a carriage over open glades and across streams, then through a woodland of oak and beech trees. Oh! You had forgotten how beautiful it all was.

Your uncle lives in a comfortable wooden house. You settle into a comfortable, cozy bedroom. You enjoy helping him organize his finances and estates. On the weekends you travel to tournaments with him.

"Next week we go falconing," your uncle says one bright spring day.

First you travel to see a man who breeds and raises birds for falconry. This is all new to you. But he offers to train you in the art. Falconry is training large birds to hunt for you. You have heard of it, but you have never seen it done before.

You are fitted with a glove upon which a hooded falcon sits. When the hood is taken from the bird's head, the bird strikes out and kills another bird or small animal and brings it back to you. It's an easy and quick way to hunt. The bird does all the work.

Your uncle is an excellent falconer, so you just watch him on the following Sunday. You are not sure you will ever be good at it.

Your uncle's falcon is like a hawk with excellent eyesight, a short hooked bill, long pointed wings, and strong legs with hooked claws. You can tell that your uncle is very fond of his falcons.

After a day of watching falconers and their falcons, you decide you like it. You will continue to learn falconry.

As the year draws to a close, you find you cannot return to the classroom. You enjoy this kind of life too much. You have met a young person who lives at the manor next door to your uncle. You will be married soon. You will have a manor of your own and live the kind of life your uncle enjoys.

You often wonder what it would have been like to teach literature at the university. But you never really know if you would have enjoyed it or not.

■ *Turn to page 109.*

London

London, England, is one of the world's largest cities. It began in A.D. 43, when the Romans built a town called Londinium and a bridge across the Thames. Thousands of people moved to London. Then, when the Romans left, Londinium was deserted. About 500 years later, William the Conqueror built a tower on the ruins of Londinium. And that was the beginning of the new London, which has continued to grow ever since.

Matching

_____ 1. Early name of London

_____ 2. River that flows through London

_____ 3. First people to establish a city on the site of London

_____ 4. These animals fought dogs for the amusement of Londoners.

_____ 5. King who built a tower on the ruins of Londinium

a) William the Conqueror

b) Romans

c) boars

d) Londinium

e) Thames

Group Activities

1. On a large map of London, find the following places:

    Hyde Park

    Thames

    Regents Park

    Tower of London

    Trafalgar Square

    No. 10 Downing Street

    Buckingham Palace

2. Discuss the recreations of Londoners in the medieval period. What do their pastimes tell you about these people?

3. Discuss the system that allowed students to not attend classes if they did not like the teacher, thus causing the teacher to lose his or her job. Would this be good or bad for education? Explain.

Individual Activities

1. Draw a picture of the Tower of London.

2. Common birds used for falconry were the peregrin falcon and the kestrel. Look up one of these, write a paragraph about it, and draw a picture of it.

3. Does the London of 1190 sound nicer or not as nice as the place where you live? Explain your answer in one or two paragraphs.

When Great Adventure Called—1270

MARCO POLO

You live in Italy when hundreds of young people like you have been going on the Crusades. This has been going on for the past two hundred years. Now a new crusade is forming to take the city of Jerusalem away from the Islamic government and give it to the Christians.

"You know," says a friend of yours, "we Christians should be able to visit Jerusalem. That is where Jesus walked. It is not fair to keep us out of there. The Turks who own Jerusalem now just won't let us in. That is why this Crusade is so important."

Your father went on a Crusade when he was young. He lost part of his arm in battle. He almost lost his life. Your grandfather went on a Crusade, too. He never came back. He died on some distant battlefield. You shake your head and say to your friend, "These Crusades seem to just go on and on. Nothing comes of them except people getting killed."

"Yes," your friend agrees. "I know it's discouraging. But think of it this way. Many Crusaders have had great adventures. They saw lands they never would have seen. Some got rich, too. We serve the Christian faith and we might have the adventure, and riches of a lifetime thrown in besides!"

You are tempted to go on the Crusade. It does sound like a good idea. But something else calls you, too. There's a young fellow in Venice named Marco Polo. He will soon be leaving on a journey across Asia to China. What an incredible adventure that would be! You would see all those strange and mysterious Eastern lands. And it would not be as dangerous as going on a Crusade, where you might be killed in battle.

■ *If you go on the Crusade, turn to page 113.*

■ *If you join Marco Polo's expedition, turn to page 114.*

Find out what your fate is!

In the end, you believe it is your duty to go on the Crusade. Your parents are surprised when you tell them your plans.

"I am going with King Louis (9th) on the Eighth Crusade," you say. King Louis of France also led the Seventh Crusade. He was defeated and captured. But then he was freed. Now he is going to fight against the Islamic Sultan of Egypt and you shall be with him.

"Ah," says your father, "I remember when we set out to save Jerusalem. We had fine metal armor and noble boys. We fought the Turks. Thirty thousand Turkish soldiers were against us. The Turks rode fine horses. They blew trumpets. Ah . . . the dust clouds were thick as our armies clashed that day. The bodies piled up like leaves after a big wind."

"Don't speak of it anymore," pleads your mother. She doesn't want to see you go. But how your father loves to talk about his war stories. The Crusade he went on is his favorite story. He is so proud of it.

"The air filled with shrieks," your father goes on. "How the javelins shone in the sun! Arrows flew through the air. We won the mighty battle against a powerful foe! It was the adventure of my life."

You get ready for your own Crusade then. On the day you gather to leave for Jerusalem, your blood pounds with excitement. Lance blades glitter in the sunshine. Brightly colored banners flash. King Louis rides at the head of your army. He is a kind man who treats all the young crusaders like a father would.

As you near Jerusalem, tragedy strikes. King Louis falls ill and dies of a fever. Then you go to the Christian stronghold at Acre in northern Palestine. There is no great battle to fight. You wait a long time. Then a truce is arranged. You can go home again.

Now you must begin your life's work. You want to be an architect. Should you study in Florence near your home or go to Spain? Magnificent building is underway there.

■ *If you go to Florence, turn to page 115.*

■ *If you go to Spain, turn to page 116.*

You decide that war is not for you. You travel to Venice and join seventeen-year-old Marco Polo and his father on the journey across Asia to Cambaluc, the capital of China. You will see the great court of Kublai Khan, grandson of the feared conquerer Genghis Khan.

You travel across the Middle East through Baghdad. Then you pass through Persia, wonderful wide plains covered with date and apple trees. Turtledoves flock by the hundreds. Sometimes the winds are so hot that you must wade in the river to escape them. But you move on.

You see so many wonders that you are delighted. The journey will take four years before you finally reach the city Kublai Khan built. Here you find his marble palace surrounded by 16 miles of parklike land, watered by springs and streams. Falcons fly overhead and deer wander tamely on the grounds.

Then you meet Kublai Khan himself. He comes riding up on a snow-white horse with a leopard lying across his saddle like a tame cat! The Kublai Khan has thousands of snow-white horses. You have never seen such marvelous creatures.

Kublai Khan is fair skinned with black eyes. He isn't very tall. Somehow you expected he would be taller. You are invited with the Polos to join him in a great banquet.

There are 40,000 other guests at the banquet! Many sit on carpeted floors. There aren't enough tables. The guests spill out into the parklike grounds; it is as if a city has descended upon the palace.

You have mare's milk and camel's milk to drink, and delicious venison and fruits of every kind to eat. It is surely the most incredible banquet you have been to in you life, or ever expect to go to!

The Kublai Khan invites you to join him the next day when he and his party go hunting. Or would you prefer to see the countryside with a small group of his royal aides?

■ *If you go on the hunt, turn to page 117.*

■ *If you visit the countryside, turn to page 118.*

You decide to go to Florence and find work on a great cathedral that is being built. You learn Gothic architecture at the side of a true master. The cathedral is tall. The arches soar up. Rays of sunlight pour through high, magnificent stained glass windows. "You see," explains the master, "all of the building is designed to lift the mind and heart to the heavens!"

You become a stone carver, making figures of saints, demons, and imps. You enjoy being part of the team building the cathedral. Sometimes you watch the architect directing all the other activities. The cranes, scaffolding, ladders, and tools are used by skilled people, but the architect runs it all.

First the architect makes plans, and then the stones are cut. The architect you work with was once a stonemason. You hope to someday be an architect, too. You shape some of the building stones. But mostly you make decorations.

All the other stonemasons who work here are educated like you. Everyone can read and write Latin and the local language.

You are paid a good wage. The architects are paid even more. The architect gets free clothing, food, candles, firewood, and his wages.

You are especially proud of your stone angels. Some stone carvers make angels that look a little bit unreal. But your angels are funny and they look like real little children. That is because, like many artists, you use real children as models. Every time you begin work, little ragged children gather around to watch you. There is nothing more interesting to a child than to see somebody make something. So the children watch you and you look at them and you copy their little faces onto the angel bodies.

Hundreds of years after you finish your work, people will still marvel at this cathedral. You don't think about this as you work. All you know is that you have found the kind of work you love.

And you are very happy about that.

■ *Turn to page 119.*

You travel to Spain, where a magnificent castle is being built. A wealthy family will live there. The castle sits high on a hill in Segovia.

You try to become a stonemason on the team that is building the castle. "I am bright. I can read and write," you say, "and I can understand the plans."

The architect looks at you suspiciously. He thinks you are too young to be of much good. You are barely out of your teens. "I will train you at the bottom. We will go down to the quarry and I will show you how to choose the best stones," he says.

You are not eager to go to a dusty old quarry. You have already done some stone carving. You think you are ready to do skilled work. But you cannot argue with the architect. He is the boss.

You go to the quarry and, as the architect is showing you a fine, big stone, another stone slips. The boulder is heading right for you! You scramble as fast as you can. But your right hand is crushed between two giant stones.

The physician you are taken to does his best. But you lose your hand. It is too badly mangled to heal. If the hand were not removed, you would die of blood poisoning.

Your life is ruined! You are sure of it. You return to your home in Italy, full of bitterness. Who wants a one-armed stone carver?

You sit around your house, grieving over your bad luck, until one day you see two beggars walk by. One is blind and the other is lame. You feel a sudden closeness to them. You are damaged, too.

You hurry outside and ask the beggars into your house. You serve them a meal.

Soon your home is a place where the poor and the disabled can come for help. You teach some of them to read and write and get jobs. You teach others just to get along with a little help from you. You grow very busy with this work and you do not have much time left over to feel sad anymore. You are, in fact, quite happy.

■ *Turn to page 119.*

You join the large hunting party of Kublai Khan and head for the forest.

"We shall hunt wild boars, wolves, stags, and bears," says one of the hunters.

Most of the large animals will be shot with arrows, but some will be hunted with leopards and lions. You are amazed to see black- and orange-striped large cats taken to the hunt in cages. Then, when you arrive in the hunting area, the cats are let out of the cages to hunt. There are huge hounds on the hunt, too. They help track down the game.

On the way to the hunt, Kublai Khan lies on a couch inside a small wooden shelter, which is carried on the backs of four elephants. On the inside of the shelter is golden cloth. On the outside are lion skins.

"Sire!" shouts one of the barons. "There are cranes in the sky!"

Quickly the roof of the Kublai Khan's shelter is opened. He gets a good view of the cranes now.

You soon arrive at a large tent set up in the wilderness. It is big enough for thousands of people! The walls of the tent are covered with furs. The Kublai Khan will sleep here on a sable fur.

You stay in a nearby tent. It is very nice, too. It's made of lion skins as well.

It is very lovely sleeping at night on the soft furs. You never even imagined such luxury before.

You decide to remain in China and work for the Kublai Khan as an envoy. You will travel all over the empire delivering messages for him.

On one of your trips you travel to India on a large boat with 60 cabins. It's a very strong boat. There are 150 crewmen, and they assure you that even if a whale strikes the boat, it will not sink.

You spend your life in China, India, and Japan—and still you see only a few of the wonders there. You have a truly exciting time of it, though.

■ *Turn to page 119.*

You would rather explore the countryside with some of the Kublai Khan's barons.

"Let us show you how kind the Khan is," one tells you.

You are taken to the city of Khan-Balik. You meet some poor people living in small houses.

"Because these people have had bad luck," explains the baron, "the Khan cares for them. He gives them light clothing for summer and woolen clothing for winter."

You travel to another part of Khan-Balik, and you find Christians and Islamic people living there. There are many astrologers who predict the weather, as well as good and bad luck.

"Would you like to see Tibet?" you are asked.

"Oh yes," you say eagerly.

You ride for two weeks through plains and villages. You are shocked to see many towns which are burned and deserted. "What happened here?" you ask.

"Wars have raged back and forth," the baron says.

You lie down in camp that night, and the baron piles a fire high with canes (thick green logs). You have just fallen asleep when the darkness fills with terrifying sounds of popping and banging. You are sure your camp is being attacked by a large army. You leap up to see the baron smiling. "Don't worry," he says. "That is just the fire. We put cane in the fire so it makes such big noises. That scares the lions and bears away. You see, this land is filled with wild beasts of prey. They would swoop down and eat us and our horses. The popping of the canes can be heard ten miles away."

You stop up your ears with a cloth and sleep well the rest of the night.

The next day you travel through a desolate wilderness. Suddenly you are attacked by a wild band of robbers. The baron and his men fight bravely, but you are killed that day.

■ *Turn to page 119.*

Gothic Style

During the Middle Ages, thousands of churches were built using Gothic style architecture. Many of these churches had large stained-glass windows. Pieces of colored glass were held together by lead strips and set into window frames. When sunlight passed through the windows, people felt as if they were walking through rainbows of color. It was like being bathed in many radiant colors. Doing stained glass was long, painstaking work. But some of these incredible works of art have lasted well over five hundred years.

True/False

_____ 1. The Crusades were fought to save China.

_____ 2. The Fourth Crusade was the last one.

_____ 3. In stained glass windows, colored glass pieces were held together by lead strips.

_____ 4. Gothic architecture was popular in the Middle Ages.

_____ 5. Marco Polo came from Florence.

Group Activities

1. On a large map find where the major Crusades were fought. Find the path Marco Polo followed to the East.

2. Discuss the spirit of adventure that led young people on journeys like Marco Polo's and even on the Crusades. Where can young people find such adventure today?

3. Make drawings of birds and fish on a thin piece of white paper. Color the surface with many colors. Draw heavy black marks around segments of the picture, as if you are making a jigsaw puzzle. Put these papers in the window where the sun can shine through and it will look like stained glass.

Individual Activities

1. In your town or city there may be churches and temples that have stained glass windows. Look at them and, if possible, see how they look from the inside when the full sun is shining.

2. Find out who owns Jerusalem today. Write the answer.

3. Look up the word *khan* in a dictionary. Write the definition.

Samurai Decision— 1272

You are a young samurai warrior in Japan. You follow a strict code which is called *Bushido*, the way of the warrior. It tells what you should and should not do. Above all you must be loyal and willing to sacrifice for your country.

You are from a noble family in Japan. Your most prized possession is your large two-handed sword. It is razor sharp. Once it belonged to your father. Now you must carry it with honor.

You have a beautiful estate in the countryside. Many peasants work your land. The law explains all your duties towards them and what they must do for you. You must treat your peasant workers fairly. They must work hard and give you total loyalty.

Long ago, as you walked through the rich rice fields with your father, he explained, "We are tough and honorable people. The samurai is one who serves society by keeping order. Watch closely that you never dishonor your position."

Now you step out on your fine porch and admire the wildly beautiful flowers blooming in your garden. Wild geese cry overhead.

Suddenly your peace is disturbed. An old peasant warns you that your neighbor—a greedy and dishonest man—has accused you of plotting against the governor!

Seizing your sword you stride to your neighbor's estate. "Withdraw the lie you made against me!" you cry.

Your neighbor attacks you with his own sword! You defend yourself, slashing his arm! You have every right to kill him, but should you instead show mercy?

━━━━━━━━━━━━━━━━━━━━

■ *If you kill him, turn to page 123.*

■ *If you spare him, turn to page 124.*

Find out what your fate is!

If you allow your enemy to live, it will only be a matter of time before he strikes again! You grasp your shorter sword and kill him. This is the first time your samurai sword has taken a life.

When the man is dead, many accounts of his past misdeeds come to life. He planned treason against the government, and that is why he accused you. It was a trick to remove suspicion from himself. He was greedy for profits, and he even sent his peasants to steal animals from other estates.

Still, you are very sorry this whole sad incident happened. You are sorry to see the wicked man's widow and children punished because of him. It is the law of the province that, in the case of treason, the entire family must share the guilt. So the widow and children lose their land.

You help the family as much as you can. But the law is the law. It seems unjust, but you are told it keeps many men from being traitors. When they know their wives and children will also suffer if they are caught, they do not commit treason.

As you try to recover from the miserable event, another problem arises. The Mongol soldiers of Kublai Khan, grandson of the fierce conquerer Genghis Khan, have sent an invasion fleet from Korea.

Japan must go to war at once to repel the invaders. As a samurai warrior, you join the defending forces. You fight bravely and suffer an almost fatal chest wound. You must spend many months recovering, but the Mongol invaders have been driven off.

In 1281, as you and your spouse raise your children on your estate, disaster strikes again. The Mongol invaders return. Should you once again join the defending forces? You still suffer pain from your war injury. You have family obligations now. You are not as young as you were when you last went to war. But you are a samurai warrior and Japan needs help.

■ *If you go, turn to page 125.*

■ *If not, turn to page 126.*

You decide to spare the wicked fellow. Perhaps having come so close to death will cause him to change his ways.

"Mend your ways and repent of your lies," you tell him sternly. "As your wound mends, may your heart and soul also improve."

You return to your own home as a sudden gust of wind blows across the land. You stop to stare at the distant mountains that are wrapped in cotton-thick clouds.

Your aunt is a poet and you love poetry, too. You sometimes read the words she has written to soothe your troubled heart. She writes about the courtly life and humanity in general. Your aunt also writes novels. She can describe nature very vividly. It makes you feel as if you are right there seeing what she sees.

Now you sit on your veranda and read for a while as clouds gather in the sky. The sun is darkened and rain begins to fall in great pelting drops.

You sleep restlessly that night. You cannot forget the bitter confrontation with your neighbor. Then, suddenly, you hear strange, disturbing sounds. You jump up and dress, grasping your sword. You push open the door and stare into the darkness.

You see shadows out in your yard near your fields. Strangers are out there. Your own peasants would not sneak around in the darkness like that.

You think immediately of your neighbor. In his rage against you for wounding him, has he sent enemies into your fields? They could be harming your animals or fouling your well.

You want to rush forward, sword in hand, to drive the shadowy figures off your land. But what if there are a great many of them? Perhaps the wiser course would be to rouse your own peasants and go to investigate the strangers with help at your side.

■ *If you rush into the yard alone, turn to page 127.*

■ *If you get help first, turn to page 128.*

You ignore your own fear and pain and go at once to battle.

Thousands of ships have brought 150,000 Mongol warriors to your shores. What fierce fighters they are! For seven weeks you are locked in desperate battle against the Mongols. You swing your sword until you can hardly lift your arm. Long beloved comrades fall at your sides. It's the most awful, bloodiest battle you have ever seen. It is hand-to-hand, sword-to-sword combat to the death. Mounted samurai warriors with bows and arrows have gone before you, but most are now slain along with their noble horses. It is up to you and those few samurai still alive to fight off the invaders.

A screaming Mongol warrior comes at you and you strike him a fierce blow. Then another comes. You cannot stand much longer. There are just too many of these Mongols. As you kill one wave of Mongol warriors, fresh warriors come in from the ships standing near the shore. The bitter truth is that the victory will go to the Mongols because there are more of them than there are samurai warriors.

Suddenly, an unexpected thing happens. The clouds above you darken. A great wind begins to blow. You have never felt such a powerful wind. You stare out to sea at a truly amazing sight.

The wind is tossing the Mongol ships about like toys. Thousands of fresh Mongol warriors who had come to attack you are dying at sea. Others, in ships still seaworthy, are fleeing before the wind.

The Mongol warriors now fighting you see the disaster, too. They lose heart. You and the other samurai warriors fight with renewed spirit. The tide of battle turns. You have a great victory!

After the last Mongol invaders are dead, you and your comrades rest on the bloody beach. You all fought bravely, but it was the wind that saved you. You call the wind the *Kamikaze* (divine wind), and you believe that heaven saved you this day.

■ *Turn to page 129.*

         Choosing Your Way Through the World's Medieval Past

Your wound from the last battle weakens you too much so you do not go to war. Soon you hear that tens of thousands of Mongol warriors are storming ashore. They come in a fleet with 4,500 ships!

"The samurai are outnumbered!" you groan to your spouse. "I must go after all!"

"No, you will only perish and do Japan no good," pleads your spouse.

But there is no choice. You rush to the battle scene to find that the tide of battle is going against the samurai.

"There is no chance for us," another samurai tells you. "We fight the Mongol warriors, then fresh ones come ashore from the ships. There are always more of them and fewer of us!"

A Mongol warrior fires his bow and the arrow strikes you in the neck. Your armor could not spare you this severe injury. Your comrades drag you behind a mound of earth. You know that death is near.

Oh, but death is not your greatest worry. The Mongol warriors are about to triumph! When they kill all the samurai warriors they will sweep across Japan. Your beloved homeland is doomed. Your family is in peril.

Then, suddenly, a great wind rises up. You have seen many winds in your life, but this is different. Your eyes are dimmed with pain, but still you see the amazing sight of Mongol ships being torn to pieces by the wind. Other Mongol ships flee. Thousands of Mongol warriors who had planned to invade are drowned!

The tide of the battle turns in your favor. The samurai warriors defeat the suddenly frightened and dispirited Mongols. The wind has accomplished this. The wind is called *Kamikaze,* or divine wind.

Before you die you have the consolation of seeing victory. Now you may die in peace.

■ *Turn to page 129.*

You rush forward with your sword to drive off the prowlers. It seems clear to you that your wicked neighbor has sent these intruders.

But you did not dream there were eight of them! You are seized and beaten by the men before you can do anything. The cowards are disguised but you recognize them as peasants who work for your neighbor. You are now sorry you didn't slay the man when you had the chance. You are left lying in field dung (manure).

You are dishonored by this shameful event. You cannot remain in the province and hold your head up high. You allowed your enemy to make a fool of you.

You leave your land in the care of your brother and hurry to another, more distant province.

You are in great economic difficulty now. What can you do to support yourself?

The Chinese are using new sailing equipment—such as the compass and cloth sails rather than slatted bamboo sails that they used to use. This might be your answer.

You learn the art of sailing and you become a pirate. How sad it is that a once noble samurai warrior was shamed into such a life. But you are successful in your new career. What is even more important, you are serving Japan in an important way.

China is your rival and your enemy. You only attack Chinese ships. Then you return to Japanese ports with booty. In a way you are still a samurai warrior, doing your share to weaken an enemy.

You once more enjoy the good things in life at your home in a booming city. You spend your free time reading sad poetry and regretting the misfortunes of your life.

■ *Turn to page 129.*

You return to your house and get your brother and several servants to arm themselves. Then all of you go out to check on the intruders.

They turn out to be peasants from the land of your wicked neighbor. You capture them and bind them. You turn them over to the Protector of the Province. Then you present evidence against your neighbor.

"He attempted to ruin my good name with lies. He sent ruffians to attack my fields and they would have probably murdered me," you say with anger.

Your neighbor loses his land and is banished. His peasants suffer the penalty of being branded in the face.

You settle down then to a few years of peace. Then the Mongol invaders attack Japan. You would go to fight against them, but your great reputation in the province has made you an important person. You are too busy settling disputes and offering advice to the emperor.

You are overjoyed when news comes that a great typhoon came up and blew the Mongol invaders into the sea. The victory has gone to the great samurai warriors, and your beloved homeland is saved.

As you grow older, you gain more land and power. You and your spouse have four children, all of whom bring honor to your household.

In the fourteenth century your family will produce a wonderful playwright who will write the popular *noh* plays. These will be called the greatest art form of the century. Your grandchildren are artists and warriors. And all of them are proud to remember you.

■ *Turn to page 129.*

Noh Plays

Japanese *noh* plays are performed on an almost empty stage with little scenery or props. But the actors, always men, wear very complicated masks. The masks portray ghosts, historical figures, religious symbols, or women if there is a woman's role in the play. A chorus chants part of the story. There is dancing, flute playing, and drum beating, too.

Matching

_____ 1. The samurai code

_____ 2. Japanese plays performed on almost empty stages

_____ 3. Samurai weapon

_____ 4. All the actors wore these to portray a wide variety of characters

_____ 5. Group that chanted part of the story in a play

a) chorus

b) masks

c) *Bushido*

d) sword

e) *noh*

Group Activities

1. Make masks as simple or complex as you want, but be sure they clearly show a character such as a skeleton, ghost, or animal. Perform a simple play using the masks.

2. Flower arranging is an old Japanese art. It is called *ikebana*. Find an encyclopedia showing how to make a simple *ikebana* arrangement, and make it in the classroom.

3. In Japan there is a special holiday honoring children. It is May 5 and it is called Children's Day. If there was such a holiday in America, what kinds of activities would you suggest for that day?

Individual Activities

1. In a history book or an encyclopedia, find a picture of a samurai warrior. Using the picture as a guide, make a drawing of your own.

2. Read some *haiku*. These are short Japanese poems. If possible, write a *haiku* poem.

3. Find a sample of Japanese calligraphy and copy a small portion of it.

Medieval Craftsperson— 1313

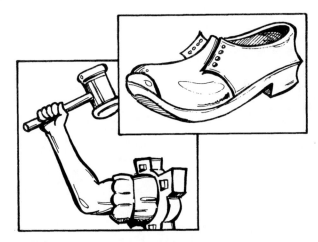

You are a youngster in your early teens. You must have a craft soon. You will become an apprentice and learn a craft. Your father died when you were very young, so he cannot help you find a craft. Your mother tells you to choose work that will please you. She says, "The work that you do has a lot to do with your happiness in life. If you must spend your life doing work you dislike, then life will lose its flavor for you."

There is a kindly shoemaker in town who is looking for an apprentice. Would you like to make shoes for a living? People always need good shoes, so you would never be idle. But the idea of making shoes, does not thrill you very much.

You have always admired the work of goldsmiths. What beautiful objects they create. The goldsmith in your town needs an apprentice. But he is well known as a cruel man. He is so mean that even his dog ran away from him. And everybody knows that a dog is the very last to abandon someone.

When you become an apprentice, you will have to spend seven long years with the master craftsman. He will provide room, board, clothing, and training. You will have to obey his commands. Then you will be a journeyman. Only then will you receive wages. After that you may become a master. Then you will have a shop of your own.

You have a very hard time deciding what to do. Should you spend seven miserable years with a tyrant like the goldsmith and then be able to do work you enjoy? Or should you spend seven pleasant years with a fine man like the shoemaker and then spend a lifetime at work you don't like?

■ *If you become an apprentice with the shoemaker, turn to page 133.*

■ *If you become an apprentice with the goldsmith, turn to page 134.*

Find out what your fate is!

You have heard that the goldsmith is so cruel he may not even let you finish your apprenticeship. So you decide to go to the shoemaker.

The shoemaker gives you a nice room in his own house to live in. He allows you to eat meals with his family. Every day you enjoy freshly baked bread with butter and fresh meat and good vegetables. The shoemaker's wife makes wonderful mince pies as well. You feel as if you are living in the home of your own grandfather.

You learn to cut leather and sew it. You make many mistakes at first, but the shoemaker is very patient. Slowly you become more skilled. Now you are ready to make your first pair of shoes. These are to be for a lady in town who wants her shoes to be very pretty. She is a bit vain.

When the shoes are finished, the lady admires them. "Excellent shoes," she says. "They will go well with my dresses."

But the next day the lady brings the shoes back! "I cannot walk comfortably in these shoes," she says. "There must be something wrong with how they are made."

You examine the shoes for defects, but there are none. The master shoemaker examines them, too. "These are well-made shoes," he says.

The woman snorts and sniffs. She is used to having everything her own way. The shoemaker must return her money, but he doesn't blame you.

Still, you are miserable. You tell the kindly shoemaker that you must find another craft. He understands and lets you go. But now what can you do? A friend of yours is a mummer, an actor in plays. That sounds like fun. Another friend is an acrobat. Could you learn to do that?

Even when you were very small you loved to entertain people.

■ *If you become a mummer, turn to page 135.*

■ *If you become an acrobat, turn to page 136.*

You grit your teeth and go to the goldsmith's shop.

"Do you know," the goldsmith says sternly, "that goldsmithing is the most respected of all the crafts?" He has a very long nose that wiggles when he talks. His nose looks like a hairy carrot.

"Oh yes, sir," you say. Already you are trembling before the strange, angry-faced man. "I have looked in the window of your shop and admired your work for many years. I long to do such work myself."

"Never!" he screams. "You are an idiot. I am a genius. No matter how long you work, you will never do work like I do. If you are lucky, you will be one half as good as I on the worst day I ever had. Remember, important noblemen and clergy-men come to me for perfection. If I take you on and you spoil my reputation, I will beat you with a stick. Is that understood?"

"Yes, yes," you mumble.

"Will you be content to sleep on straw in the corner of the workshop? I surely will not allow you into my home. And will you be pleased with cold porridge, and meat only on Sundays and feast days? I cannot waste good food on an apprentice who probably will not work out in the end," says the goldsmith.

"I will be glad for anything," you say. But you are getting less sure of your decision by the minute.

"Will you work 12 hours a day at least, and not complain if sometimes you must work all night?" demands the goldsmith.

"Yes," you whisper. You are fearful now that you made a terrible mistake. Why, you will be living worse than a slave!

"And if I must take a stick to you, you swear you will not go complaining about me?" asks the goldsmith. A master craftsman who abuses his apprentice can be punished by the guilds. But if you swear never to complain, what will become of you if you are mistreated?

You have a great desire to escape this awful place while there is still time.

■ *If you leave, turn to page 137.*

■ *If you remain, turn to page 138.*

You decide that being a mummer would be the most fun. So you join your friend's acting company. They are doing a religious play called *The Castle of Perseverance.*

"Where is the play performed?" You imagine that a religious play would be performed in the churchyard.

"Oh, we perform in the pageant wagon," explains your friend. "In the bottom of the wagon we put on our costumes. The top level of the wagon is the stage. Everyone gathers around the wagon and there we are doing the play way up high where everybody can see us."

"Is there a big part for me in this play?" you ask.

Your friend laughs. "What big ideas you have! No, you must start small as we all did. You must do a lot of work like set up the stage and feed the horses that pull the wagon. Then you get to blow a little trumpet to let everybody know that I am coming on stage. I play the part of the world, you see."

"How do you play the world?" you want to know.

"I am crowned with gold and dressed in ermine, a fine fur. I am seated on a gilded throne. When I am announced as the world and you blow the trumpet, I come in with great leaps and sit on my throne before everybody. Folly and greed pay me honor."

"Can't I play folly or greed?" you ask.

"No," says your friend. "Just blow the trumpet!" You are disappointed, but what can you do?

At the time of the performance, you blow your trumpet with all your breath. Then you help sew up costumes and put oil on the wagon wheels. You don't get to do any real acting for six months. Then, at last, you get the chance to play the devil.

Your costume, made of black leather, has horns and hooves. You even have an evil-looking pitchfork to carry.

You shout out your lines on the night of the performance, "I champ, I chase, I chock on my chin!" you scream. You are a frightening devil. Everybody says so. You become a member of the actors guild, and this will be your life.

You are delighted with your choice. You doubt that anybody has more fun at their work than you do.

■ *Turn to page 139.*

You practice swinging on ropes and chandeliers. You leap across chasms and gaps. You turn and jump and perform somersaults. You also practice tumbling. Then you set out for the country fair to see if you are good enough to make a living doing this.

The sun is shining brightly as you arrive. A fellow is standing there juggling for a crowd. He is throwing up balls, batons, and clubs. Then he throws up fruit and flaming brands. It's very exciting. Everybody is cheering and clapping. You are surprised how good he is.

Finally the fellow starts throwing up knives. It looks dangerous! He would be badly cut if he caught one at the blade instead of the handle. The crowd is very silent. They seem to like dangerous tricks the best. But the juggler never misses.

What a fine performance! The crowd showers the man with coins. He has done very well. Now it's your turn. You are lucky that a good crowd is already gathered.

You begin to tumble. You hear laughter. Oh no! They are laughing at you!

"Look at the clumsy thing! I could do as well when I was ten," somebody says.

You decide to switch to another of your skills. You throw a rope over the nearby tree branch. You swing from it. The laughter grows louder. You'd better do more somersaults.

End over end you go.

"Bring the juggler back!" the crowd chants. "This fool is not good."

You scramble away with a rotten piece of fruit striking your back. How cruel they are!

"You there," calls a pig trader. "Would you help me herd my hogs? They've gotten away in the brush. There will be two pennies for you if you get them all back."

You catch the pigs and collect your two pennies. Perhaps if you hang around the country fairs you will always be able to make a few pennies at such tasks. It's far from what you dreamed of, but it's a living.

■ *Turn to page 139.*

You cannot bear so much suffering! You turn on your heel and hurry away.

You find that the shoemaker already has an apprentice now. So you wander about for four days looking for something else. Then you are hired by a wagoner who travels from town to town selling pots and pans and other useful products. He is old and he needs a young person to help him handle the mules and repair the wagon wheels when they break.

You earn only a penny a day, and it seems you spend half your time loading and unloading the wagon when it breaks down. Each time you lose a wheel you must unload the wagon and hoist it up to fix it.

Life is dull and full of boring hard work. But you cannot find anything better, so you travel for three years with the old man.

"I shall be giving this up," the old man tells you one day. "You may have my wagon and my household goods, youngster."

Now the broken-down wagon and the pots and pans belong to you. You pick up the route. You travel from town to town just as the old man did. You get to know the people living in the tiny villages and the countryside.

When the farm families see you coming, they run to your wagon to see if you have anything new. Sometimes you enjoy some sweet cake and a glass of cider with a customer. Sometimes they even invite you inside to warm yourself by their fires.

You never make much money, but it's a pleasant life. You don't work too hard and you make some friends along the way. But sometimes you wonder what it would have been like to have become a goldsmith.

Did you give up on your dream too easily?

■ *Turn to page 139.*

Though your legs are shaking, you agree to everything.

You are shown to a pile of dirty straw in the corner. You don't sleep very well that night, but you are shaken awake at dawn. You must quickly eat your cold porridge. Ugh, how awful it tastes!

The goldsmith orders you to cover a clay model with wax. Then you cover it with plaster. The plaster has holes in it. When the model is heated, the wax melts and flows out through the holes.

You watch the goldsmith pour melted bronze into the holes. The bronze cools and hardens and the shell is broken away. A beautiful bronze object remains!

It takes you three months to even make a bronze doorknob to the goldsmith's satisfaction. He yells at you a hundred times every day. But you think your doorknob is quite good.

After a year of miserable living and much abuse (though he never hits you with the stick he always waves over your head), you at last begin to work with gold. You engrave a design into a gold plate with a tool called a burin, a steel knife-like tool with a sharp point.

The goldsmith comes over and examines your work. "It is less terrible than I expected," he mutters.

From this goldsmith, that is high praise! Your spirits soar.

You continue to grow in the skills of a goldsmith. In the second year the master only yells at you half as much. In the third year he only yells about twice a day.

And then the time comes when the goldsmith comes to examine a golden cup you have made. He does not say anything for a long time. Then he says, "Good."

You could shout for joy. He has never said good before! The time flies now. Before you know it you are a journeyman. And then you are a master with your own workshop. From your workshop come some of the most beautiful objects of gold in all of Europe. And you are filled with joy. You are doing what you love. Long ago you have forgiven the cruel goldsmith. Now you feel quite warm towards him.

■ *Turn to page 139.*

■ *Turn to page 139.*

Entertainment in the Middle Ages

For entertainment in medieval times, people went to the country fairs and watched jugglers, tumblers, and other performers. Sometimes they went to alehouses (restaurants) and listened to minstrels (singers), comedians, and storytellers.

Medieval plays were all religious. They were performed in large travel wagons or sometimes in the fields. They were exciting and colorful, but they always taught a moral lesson, too. Good and evil always appeared in the plays, and the audience was supposed to go home not only entertained but improved.

True/False

_____ 1. If you were learning a craft you were called an apprentice.

_____ 2. Before you became a master you were a journeyman.

_____ 3. Medieval plays were not often religious plays.

_____ 4. Medieval plays all taught a lesson.

_____ 5. Apprentices had to serve for two years.

Group Activities

1. Discuss the apprentice system. Was it good for young people? Was it better or worse than the present system of going to school and learning a trade?

2. Discuss entertainment in the Middle Ages. How did it differ from entertainment in our lives? Was it harder or easier to find entertainment?

3. Find a medieval play like *Everyman* and do a short portion of it in class.

Individual Activities

1. In medieval times one craftsperson made a shoe from start to finish. Now many people do various parts of the process in shoemaking. In one or two paragraphs, give your opinion on which way was more interesting for the person making the shoe.

2. Find information about one of the following people. Write a paragraph describing who he was and what he did.

   a) Chaucer   b) Dante Alighieri

3. In one paragraph describe either the shoemaker or the goldsmith.

In the Empire of Mali—1332

You live in the empire of Mali in northwestern Africa. Mali has been an important gold-exporting empire for 300 years. Your own great grandfather was a personal friend of the famous Mali king Baramendana Keita. Your present ruler, Mansa Musa, is a fine king. He is managing the empire well. Your parents have told you so.

The empire of Mali stretches from the Atlantic Ocean on the west to the region of modern Nigeria on the east. As a youngster here, you are proud of your land. Now it's time for you to think about what you will do when you are an adult.

Your mother thinks you should go to the learning center in the city of Timbuktu. "You have a good mind. You could study law. Trained lawyers will be needed," she says. "You have always been good at settling arguments between your brothers and sisters."

Your uncle leads trade caravans using camels north across the Sahara, all the way to the Mediterranean Sea. You have always dreamed of going on one of those caravans. Maybe then, after such an adventure, you would be ready to start studying law. But right now you are very restless. Books and study do not appeal to you.

"Don't be foolish," warns your father (who usually agrees with your mother). "The desert is wild and dangerous. When your uncle weaves his tales of great adventure, he leaves out the miseries of the desert heat and wind. He does not mention what would happen to you if the Tuareg tribesmen attack. The sensible decision is to go at once to school so that you might soon begin your career. You are not a child anymore."

You know that your parents are right. But when you are settled down with a family and a career, there will be no time anymore for adventure!

■ *If you go on the trade caravan, turn to page 143.*

■ *If you go to school immediately, turn to 144.*

Find out what your fate is!

Your parents have decided not to argue when you tell them you want to get in one big adventure before you settle down to study. So you hurry to watch the camels being loaded down with gold, kola nuts, and leather goods. You can feel the excitement in the air. Your uncle grins at you and says, "Life is good in Mali. But there will be plenty of time for you to study law and find a comfortable house near the mosque when you are older. Now you are still a youngster. You must see faraway places." Your uncle understands what it is to be young even though he is older.

You find riding a camel very strange at first, but you get used to it. You are heading for the city of Marrakesh, the starting point for caravans crossing the Sahara. The camels move at a steady pace. Your uncle says, "When all goes well we can cover a great distance in a week. We go about 200 miles. This journey of 1,000 miles usually takes five weeks. That will depend on the wells being full. It will depend on the oases not failing."

"What if we come to a dry well?" you ask.

"Then the caravan must turn to find another place where there is water. It will cause delay," says your uncle.

You watch the vegetation thin out until there is only sand. What a strange, beautiful sight the great sand dunes present. They are like waves frozen on a sea.

You are moving towards an oasis that your uncle says has never failed him. But when you reach it, the small lake is dry. A look of deep worry comes to your uncle's face.

"We must now turn sharply east where I know of a well. But that will delay us, and what is worse, Tuareg tribesmen use the well. We could be running into trouble if we go there. If we go straight ahead, we shall come to another oasis, but if that is dry, too, we could die on the desert. Shall we risk going ahead and trust that the second oasis has not failed? Or shall we face the Tuaregs and a long delay?" asks your uncle.

■ *If you turn east, turn to page 145.*

■ *If you go straight ahead, turn to page 146.*

Though you would much rather be going on the camel caravan, you take your parents' advice and head for school.

"We are very lucky to have such a fine center of learning," says your teacher when you arrive. "We can thank King Mansa Musa for bringing the Islamic scholars into the empire so we might learn from them."

At school you study the Koran (the holy book of Islam) and other books as well. You hear lectures from the Book of *Maghrib* by Ibn-Said, a North African historian. You hear about the magnificent Islamic kingdom in Spain.

You also study algebra, geometry, and trigonometry. But the best thing about being at school is the chance to discuss important ideas with really intelligent people.

You will be a lawyer, so you are pleased to hear that the master science of the Islamic world is law.

"Law molds the whole society," a teacher explains. "All private and public activities are guided by the law."

You study hard, and when you return home you are well prepared to practice law. After several years you become a judge. The first major case you are called upon to judge involves a dispute among merchants.

"This man broke the law of the Koran," says a leather merchant. "I was in need of some money to pay for my journey to Marrakesh. I asked him for help. He gave me some money. But when I returned to Timbuktu, he asked for interest on the money. The Koran forbids the taking of interest."

"No," says the other man. "All I did was expect a gift of appreciation. I did not ask for interest. I thought the ungrateful fellow would at least give me a small gift for lending him the money he needed."

You study the case. You decide the first man is in the wrong. "It is the custom to give a gift of appreciation," you tell the leather merchant. "The man you accuse did not break the law of the Koran."

Your reputation for wisdom spreads. Now you must decide whether to carry the king's message to the Ottoman Turks or settle a dispute among the king's relatives in Spain.

■ *If you go to the Ottoman Turks, turn to page 147.*

■ *If you go to Spain, turn to page 148.*

You decide to turn east toward the well your uncle has used before. It is very difficult traveling across the sand, which blows across the trails and makes it easy to get lost.

Luckily the camels don't need much water and they plod on with their heavy loads. You are frightened but you don't say anything. Maybe coming on the caravan was not such a good idea, you think. The desert is a dangerous place to be without water.

You move slowly in the scorching heat. Your uncle stares out across the sand and pointing says, "There the well must be."

"Are you sure?" you ask hopefully.

He nods. He is a brave man. He has traveled this perilous route ever since he was a boy. You are sure that not even the much-feared, black-veiled Tuareg warriors really frighten him. You are not so brave. You think longingly of the pleasant classroom in Timbuktu. You wish you were there right now.

You shout with joy when you find the well full. No Tuaregs threaten you as you gather plenty of water for the rest of the journey.

You must make another sharp turn to get back on the northwest course to Marrakesh.

You reach the hills near the coast about six weeks after starting the journey. Down below lies Marrakesh on the great plain at the foot of the mountains.

You help unload the gold, hides, and kola nuts you have brought. Then you help load the camels for the return journey. You will be carrying European cloth and other goods for the southward journey.

"I like especially the jewelry items we take back," says your uncle with a smile and a wink. "There is much profit in them and they do not load down the camels, eh?"

But the salt you carry is important, too.

It is a wonderful adventure, but you are glad when it is over. It is fun to talk about the scary parts, but you are just as happy it is all behind you as you head for school.

■ *Turn to page 149.*

You remain on course, heading for the next oasis. If only you find it green and bubbling with water!

How weary you are as you move through the harsh heat. The heat comes down from the burning sky and reflects back from the sand. It is unbearable!

Even the camels stumble in the ever-changing sand dunes.

When you reach the oasis, your heart sinks. It is dry! Fear turns to desperation. You do not ask your uncle how good your chances are of surviving. You dare not, for he will not lie to you. You can see in his dark eyes and furrowed brow that you may be doomed!

After many days in a useless search for water, your uncle frees the camels. "They cannot carry us or the goods any longer. They are themselves near the end," he says. "Let the poor beasts try to find water on their own."

You watch in horror as the valuable gold tumbles into the sand. Nothing has any meaning now!

Your uncle has begun to pray. He expects to die. He is turning his thoughts beyond death to the life he believes awaits him then. He turns to you and says, "Remember that after death there is judgment. Heaven abounds in deep rivers of cool, crystal water. . . ."

Your uncle dies peacefully soon after that. You must struggle on alone. Soon it will be your turn to die. If only you can go with as much dignity as the old man showed.

Your tongue feels like a piece of leather. You think you are choking! A great sandstorm has come up and you are blinded. You drop to your knees. Is this the end?

Suddenly you see a camel in the distance. Has one of the poor beasts you set free returned? No! It is a trade caravan moving south. You have been rescued!

The caravan has plenty of water and someone drips the cool liquid on your parched lips. Little by little you can take larger amounts of water. If you gulped it down all at once you would get violently sick.

You are almost your old self when you return home to Timbuktu. You will never forget this horrifying adventure, though. And you will grieve a long time for your brave uncle.

■ *Turn to page 149.*

You decide to carry the message to the Ottoman Turks in the city of Bursa, near the sea of Marmara in northwest Turkey.

You are well received by Suleiman, now head of the Ottoman Turks. He sends his good wishes back to the king of Mali. And now you have some free time to look around this strange new place.

You gaze at the caravansaries, which are two-story buildings for the camel caravans. On the lower floor are stables for the animals. Upstairs, goods may be stored. And what an incredible trade empire the Ottoman Turks have! Everything is so well organized.

Now it is time to see Samarkand. You are eager. You have heard so much about this great city that was destroyed by Alexander the Great over 1,700 years ago.

"You will see it has been rebuilt," says your round-faced, happy Turkish host. "It was destroyed by Genghis Khan about a hundred years ago. Then it was rebuilt again. Now it thrives."

Along the way to Samarkand you climb steep mountains. You see wild sheep with huge horns. The sheep cling to rocky outcroppings. How sure-footed these wonderful beasts are. They seem to dance in midair as they jump over canyons.

"The shepherds use the horns of the sheep to make bowls to eat from," says your host. "They even use the horns to make fences to hold their flocks."

It's so cold and high along this part of the trail that you don't even see birds for almost two weeks. Then you reach the Kashgar Pass, where there are many orchards. And then, at last, Samarkand. Islamites and Christians live here in peace. The spires of Christian churches and Islamic minarets may be seen all over.

"This city is more than 4,000 years old," says your host. "Think how many have stood where we now stand!"

You will have priceless memories of this wonderful journey. But the best memory will be of how different people lived in peace and friendship.

■ *Turn to page 149.*

You travel to Spain to settle the dispute between the distant relatives of the king. They are both silk fabric weavers in Al-Andalus (Andalusia). They are Berbers from North Africa whose ancestors came to Spain hundreds of years ago.

You go to visit the two cousins and tell them, "My king hears that there is disunity between you. It troubles him greatly."

The one cousin sits on a long couch. He rises and snatches up his fabric to show you. It is a magnificent design of brilliant red peacocks and other red objects. You must admit it is strikingly beautiful. "This I have woven with my own hands," says the man, "but my cousin says his work is superior to mine. This wounds me greatly. I feel no fabric could be more beautiful than this."

"Ah," says the other cousin (who is older), "look here at perfection!" He displays another fabric. A creature that looks like a rooster prances in a scene filled with graceful swirls and leaves. "Do you see? Is this not perfection?"

You scratch your head and try to be wise. Both fabrics are beautiful. Neither is superior to the other. Each shows the special vision of a gifted artist. No two visions are alike.

"I have studied law, not art," you tell the two cousins. "But listen to what I have learned. Material things are not important in life. The silk fabrics are beautiful, but they are only things. If you let material things divide you into angry enemies, then you are not following the straight path in life."

The cousins listen. Then they embrace one another.

"Your peacocks are marvelous," says the older cousin.

"Your rooster is excellent," says the younger cousin.

You smile, glad that you have succeeded. When you return to the king, he is delighted by your success. He immediately gives you another, even more important position.

■ *Turn to page 149.*

Askia the Great

The Songhay empire followed the empire of Mali. One of its greatest kings was Askia the Great. He was a soldier, but he studied government, taxes, trade, weights and measures, and religion so he could rule wisely. He understood how to keep the empire economically healthy. He used moral principles to guide his laws. For 36 years he was a fair and honest ruler. That was why he was called great.

Matching

_____ 1. Mansa Musa was a king of

_____ 2. Askia was king of

_____ 3. The old empire of Mali stretched from the Atlantic Ocean to modern

_____ 4. Mali's most important city was

_____ 5. He ruled for 36 years

a) Nigeria

b) Askia

c) Timbuktu

d) Songhay

e) Mali

Group Activities

1. On a map of medieval Africa find the kingdoms of Mali, Songhay, and Ghana. What countries are included in these old empires?

2. Why do you think Africa had such advanced civilizations so long ago and then, for about 500 years, there was a decline? Discuss possible reasons.

3. If you were about to settle down to train for your career but first could have an adventure, what would it be? Share your ideas in a group discussion.

Individual Activities

1. Find out who rules Mali today. Write in one or two paragraphs how the country is doing economically and politically.

2. In two paragraphs, finish the story that begins with this sentence: "I was in the middle of the Sahara with no water in sight. Suddenly I saw . . . ."

3. Find some examples of African art and copy them. Then make a poster showing some of the examples that you drew.

The Grim Reaper— 1348

It is summer in England and you work with many other youngsters in a textile mill. Some of your co-workers are eight or nine years old, though you are a bit older. You sew fabric all day in the small town where you live. Your town has narrow, dirty streets and there are rats everywhere. How it frightens you to walk home in the dark and see the large rats scurrying along beside you. Some seem as big as small-sized dogs! If you kick at any rubbish pile, surely a rat will flee.

You run up the stairs to the home you share with your parents. Your father makes shoes, though he is half blind. Your mother is a spinster, the operator of a spinning wheel. You live above the shoe shop.

Tonight your mother is very worried as she puts out bread and thin soup. "The grim reaper is coming," she says. The grim reaper means death. "So many are dying in Italy and France and now here, too. Two families in Buckinghamshire have lost children this week!"

Your mother speaks of the bubonic plague, which is called the Black Death. The disease is ravaging Europe. It is a grim reaper indeed!

Your father dips a slice of bread into the soup and stares at you. You are the only child of your parents. Your two older brothers died as infants. Your parents do not want something to happen to the only child they have left.

"I think it would be best if you went to stay with my brother in Worcestershire," your father says. Your uncle is a parish priest. "It is not so dirty and crowded there in the country. You would be safer from the disease."

"Yes," your mother agrees, "where there are rats and filth, more die."

But you don't want to leave your job here in town.

■ *If you go to Worcestershire, turn to page 153.*

■ *If you remain in town, turn to page 154.*

Find out what your fate is!

You are very sorry to give up your job. It does not pay that well, but it was nice having money of your own. But you do not want to worry your parents, so you do as they say. Also, you fear the Black Death as much as they do. What awful stories you have heard.

In Italy hundreds of thousands died in one region. In some of the smaller villages there are no people left alive to bury the dead!

You travel out to the parish church in Worcestershire, and your uncle welcomes you.

"Is it safer here from the Black Death?" you ask him.

Your uncle shrugs his shoulders. "I was told the whole Rhone River has been blessed. That is so it can serve as a graveyard. The gravediggers cannot keep up with their task. The dead must be hurled into the river," he says.

"But the Rhone River is in France, not here," you say.

"Yes. We can hope and pray. But when our time comes, it comes," says the priest.

Before too long, you hear that a family near the church has been stricken with the Black Death. You watch your uncle hurry off to give the last rites (prayers for the dying).

You fear that your uncle is in greater danger than other people. What if he catches the disease from all the sick people he prays with?

You talk about this to the farmer's daughter next door. "Ah," she says, "the priests in France and Italy were among the first to die. Who but a priest would enter a house where people were dying of the Black Death?"

You are now afraid to stay here with your uncle. You must go elsewhere. A cousin lives on a farm about 20 miles away. They would let you stay there if you worked hard. Or you might go to live with your grandparents in Ely. They could use your young hands, for they are growing old.

■ *If you go to your cousin's farm, turn to page 155.*

■ *If you go to your grandparents, turn to page 156.*

You have heard that priests are getting the Black Death quicker than other people because they are always going among the sick. You are as safe to stay where you are and keep on working.

In the days ahead, two of your co-workers get chills and fever. Then blotches and boils cover their bodies! They are sick only a few days before they die. You are terror-struck. You and all the others who work at the shop flee. You shall never return. But maybe it is already too late.

You and your parents pack all your belongings in a wagon and flee to the countryside. You leave everything. Your father even leaves many of his tools in the shoe shop.

As your wagon rattles along, you see abandoned farms. You shudder to think that an entire family probably died there. Cattle roam in the field with nobody to watch them. Crops are rotting on the vines because nobody is alive to pick them. In one field you see the rotting bodies of thousands of sheep who have died, maybe of the plague, too!

You pass a large monastery. An old monk is outside tending the land.

"Has the Black Death struck here?" your father asks.

The monk nods. "Ten of the monks have died," he says. You hurry on. Is everyone doomed? Is the world coming to an end?

You reach a small village. There are no people in it. Everyone has run away or died. You keep moving.

"We must travel deep into the forest and live on wild game and berries," says your father.

"No, no," your mother says. "Just ahead there is a small village. I lived there as a girl. I know some people there who will help us. We cannot live in the forest like savages."

■ *If you go to the forest, turn to page 157.*

■ *If you stop in the village, turn to page 158.*

You arrive at your cousin's farm in the country. You are glad to see dirt roads free of rubbish. It looks so much healthier here than it did in town. You are soon at work helping with the farm chores. You collect eggs and churn butter from the milk. You are suddenly full of hope that the Black Death cannot reach you here.

One day you are raking hay in the barn when a large rat races across your shoe. You turn white with fear. "There are rats in the barn," you tell your cousin in a trembling voice.

"Yes. There are rats everywhere," says your cousin. "Just as there are flies everywhere."

"Some say the rats carry the Black Death," you say. "They must be shot."

"Who knows what causes the sickness?" your cousin says. "The doctor in town says it is caused by impure vapors in the air. He says the vapors enter through pores in the skin. That is why the doctor wears protective clothing when he visits the sick."

You work hard on the farm and then, one awful morning, you wake up with a fever. Oh no! You tremble in terror as you pull the covers up around your neck. "I am doomed," you whisper to yourself.

Your cousin is hysterical when you say you have a fever. "You must go! Go at once. Don't breathe on me!" your cousin screams.

As sick as you are, you drag yourself from bed. You gather your few possessions and stagger out. Your cousin burns all your bedding behind you. You are dizzy with fever as you move down the road. You must rest! You sit down against a tree in a meadow. You mumble a prayer. You hope you go to heaven as soon as you die.

Then, suddenly, you feel the warm sun on your face. You have been sleeping a long time. You are afraid to open your eyes. Will you find boils and splotches on your body?

You open your eyes. You have no marks! You feel better. It was only a passing fever after all, not the bubonic plague. You break into song as you hurry down the road. How good it feels to be alive!

■ *Turn to page 159.*

■ *Turn to page 159.*

You go to your grandparents' small cottage at the edge of a town. They are not as worried about the Black Death as you are. They have lived through many disasters. "What is destined to be, will be," says your grandmother.

The little town is quite clean compared to the town where you used to live. You help your grandmother weave cloth and help your grandfather in his small vegetable garden. Then, after about a month, your grandfather falls ill! You are terrified. You want to flee, but you cannot leave your grandmother alone.

The doctor comes and gives you the terrible news. It is the Black Death! The doctor does not even want to remain long in the house. All the time he is here he is inhaling spices through his face mask. He hopes this will cleanse the air of the plague germs.

Your grandmother then falls ill, too. You are alone, caring for your grandparents. There is little you can do. When you call the priest, he comes and gives your grandparents the last rites of the Church. They both die within a day of each other.

You are sure you are doomed, too. You bury your grandparents and then return to the sad, empty house. You go about doing your chores, just waiting for the disease to strike you down.

But winter comes and you are still well. You return to your parents' house in town. There is hope that the worst of the Black Death is over. All the mice and rats have been killed. Maybe this will help.

The Black Death returns the next year, but it is not as widespread. You are a much stronger person than you used to be. You are still well, and now you are determined to make something special out of your life.

You remember what your grandmother said: "What is destined to be will be." You think that means that your life was spared for a reason. And now you must fulfill your destiny in life.

■ *Turn to page 159.*

You live in your wagon deep in the forest. Your father shoots wild rabbits for food and you live off that and wild fruits. Your mother is very unhappy. She cannot bear this kind of living.

"We live worse than the serfs," she groans. "This sort of life is worse than death."

But your father will not listen to any argument. His fear of the Black Death is a disease in itself. He can think of nothing else. He can speak of nothing else. When he sees a mouse or a rat he kills it and burns the body.

But your father does not worry about the rabbits. He does not know that the disease-bearing fleas live on rabbits, too.

Your father is the first to grow ill. You watch the awful boils cover his body. No doctor can be called. Doctors cannot do anything anyway, and one will not come into the forest. So you and your mother do your best to comfort your father. And when he dies you pray for him and bury him in the woodland.

"We must go to the village now where my family is," your mother says. But it is too late. You already have a fever. You feel sicker than you have ever felt in your life.

As your fever rises, you remember the happy days of your childhood. You think especially of Christmas, when the house was fragrant with the smell of wild goose. How you loved the plum pudding! You remember the toys you got from your grandparents when you were seven. They were a set of miniature knights and ladies. Your grandfather bought them from a peddler.

How happy you are as the good memories flood in. Why is your mother crying so?

Your mother closes your eyes, and soon you lie beside your father in the woodland. Your mother returns to her village and tells everyone how her husband and only child died of the Black Death.

■ *Turn to page 159.*

You arrive in the village where your mother used to live. You stay with distant relatives. Your father is sure that you will all die here. But your mother and the other ladies are busy making sure the village is kept clean.

"No piles of rubbish anywhere," says your mother. "Every bit of garbage must be buried at once. Rats live in rubbish and garbage."

You sweep and burn until everything is very clean and neat. The moment you finish a meal, the leftovers must be dug deeply into the ground.

It is a tiny village with a small church. Everybody goes often to church to pray that the Black Death does not come to this village. When you are not praying, you are sweeping and cleaning.

One day your mother and two other women find a pile of rubbish at a neighbor's back door. "Indolent [lazy] wretch," screams your mother. "Do you want to raise rats that will be the death of us all?"

The frightened man quickly burns his rubbish and buries the ashes.

Nobody in the small village dies that summer of the Black Death. When winter comes, the deaths from the plague drop all over England.

The Black Death returns to England the next year, but far fewer people die. It seems the terrible scourge has begun to decline.

You and your family go to live in London. You get a job in the thriving textile industry there. After several years you save enough money to get a small shop of your own.

You marry and have six children. You often tell them how it was when you were young and the Black Death swept Europe. Their eyes grow wide when they hear your stories. And everybody ends up saying how good it is that the Grim Reaper has not come back in so awful a way again.

■ *Turn to page 159.*

■ *Turn to page 159.*

The Black Death

The bubonic plague epidemic of the Middle Ages may have killed about one third of all the population. No good statistics were kept then, but we know that in the small town of Hadeston in England, 68 out of 400 died. In a manor at Winslow, three out of five adults died. Because they always went to the homes of the sick, priests died at a higher rate than ordinary people. One half of all the priests during that time died of the Black Death. Many people feared that everybody would die eventually. Bubonic plague is caused by the bite of an infected animal or by the fleas living on that animal. This disease is rare now and it can be successfully treated.

True/False

_____ 1. Most streets in English towns in 1348 were dirty.

_____ 2. A spinster was a spinning wheel operator.

_____ 3. The Black Death was typhoid fever.

_____ 4. Some think the Black Death killed about one third of the people.

_____ 5. Fewer parish priests than other people died of the Black Death.

Group Activities

1. Discuss what was done in the stories in response to the Black Death. Would people act the same today under the same circumstances?

2. Discuss the various characters in the selections (such as parents, grandmother, priest, cousin) and how they reacted to the Black Death. Which reaction was most sensible?

3. Art was affected by the Black Death. There were sad, grim paintings during that time. Make a poster of medieval art showing fears of the Black Death, or make up your own art reflecting this feeling.

Individual Activities

1. Imagine you are living in England in 1348. In two paragraphs describe the fear of the Black Death.

2. In one paragraph, describe how one of the following groups of people reacted to the Black Death.

   a) doctors   b) priests

3. Read the old childhood rhyme "Ring around the Rosie" or "Ring-a ring o' Roses." Not many people know it referred to the Black Death. Reread it and see the connection.

The Inca Way— 1440

You are a young Inca in Peru. Your family raises barley, potatoes, and corn. You are skilled in the use of the sling. You hurl stones at birds and wild animals who try to eat your crops. Life is hard here in the mountains, especially when you go on long hunting trips. Sometimes you must live on wild potatoes and snails and lizards.

Your family are commoners. One third of all your produce goes to the family. One third goes to the government officials and craftspeople who do not raise food. The last third is stored in granaries for everyone to use when there is crop failure in the land.

You will always be a commoner. This is the class you were born into and there you will stay. The noble classes live much differently than you do. They have beautiful homes and fine clothing made from silky alpaca and vicuña wool. The nobles have gold and turquoise jewelry.

The emperor lives in a grand palace at Cuzco. He dines off gold dishes. His clothes are richly embroidered and he eats only the finest food. You have never been to Cuzco, but you admire the emperor. If you ever saw him you would bow down low before him.

Your own house has one room and no windows. It is made of adobe or mud brick with a thatched roof.

You and your brother herd your llamas, which carry goods to the lower land to trade. Your llama carries gourds to be used as bowls. Your brother's llama is loaded with silky wool.

"Look," says your brother, "let's take a shortcut."

"But the shortcut is steep and dangerous," you say.

Your brother grins. "Are you afraid?" he asks.

■ *If you avoid the steep shortcut, turn to page 163.*

■ *If you take the shortcut, turn to page 164.*

Find out what your fate is!

You decide to stay with the safer trail. You have beautiful gourd bowls with fine inlay work of stones and shells. The llama is surefooted, but if the rocks beneath his feet give way, then all your valuable goods will be spilled out and perhaps broken.

Still, you are anxious to reach the marketplace. Others have gourd bowls and wool to trade, too. If you reach the marketplace late in the day, nobody may want to buy your gourds. And the products you wish to buy will all be gone. You must have fruits and vegetables and medicinal herbs grown by the lowlanders.

"Because you were cowardly, we shall miss the best fruits and herbs," scolds your brother. "Others will have picked over everything and left the poor fruit for us."

Rushing for the last few yards, you reach the village marketplace. It is crowded with mountain people like you. You all wear coarse cloaks (called ponchos), headbands, and sandals of llama hide.

You find many still willing to buy your gourd bowls. There are still fresh, red tomatoes, sweet potatoes, peanuts, and medicinal herbs. You make excellent trades and you give your brother an "I told you so" grin.

You pass through stalls of striking pottery. These *huacos* are sculptured and painted jugs. Some are buried with the dead so they might have nice jugs in the next world.

Suddenly you see a well-dressed man with gold ear plugs carrying a large bundle. He is running with three warriors after him. A thief! You watch in horror as the thief kills a warrior and then is captured by the others. Then you are called by one of the two warriors. "You!" he shouts, "you must go to the great sun temple at Cuzco and give witness to what you saw. This man must be punished."

You would love to see Cuzco, but you are afraid to go so far from home. You are tempted to just run away.

■ *If you go to Cuzco with the warriors, turn to page 165.*

■ *If you run, turn to page 166.*

You take the steep trail and, just as you feared, the llamas lose their footing. Luckily you save the gourd bowls and, after losing precious time, repack the goods. You glare at your brother for his bad idea. Then you hurry towards the marketplace before all the fruits and vegetables you want to trade for are gone.

You reach the marketplace and trade the gourds and wool for some deliciously ripe tomatoes, sweet potatoes, and medicinal herbs. You load your llamas for the homeward journey.

Then, suddenly, a youngster races up, snatches a tomato from you, and runs.

"Thief," you and your brother scream. You attract the attention of a young warrior. He takes chase and captures the boy who stole your tomato.

"Our family is large. We cannot afford to lose even one tomato," you tell the warrior.

The warrior looks sternly at the thief. "Why did you steal?" he asks.

"Because my own family starves," the youngster says, hanging his head.

"Why do they starve? What is wrong?" asks the warrior.

"We work for a landholder. We are Yana-Cunas, farmers who rent land. Our landholder works us but then he will not give us enough to eat," says the thief.

You feel very sorry for the young thief now. You are sorry you called attention to his theft. Now he will be severely punished. You have heard of thieves being flogged until their backs were bloody, or sometimes stoned to death. It seems so unfair to punish someone for being hungry.

"It is all right. We will not miss one tomato," you say.

"The crime must be judged," says the soldier. "Come and see justice done. It will be a lesson to your young mind."

Do you dare watch some cruel punishment?

■ *If you watch it, turn to page 167.*

■ *If you continue your journey home, turn to page 168.*

You travel to Cuzco with the warriors while your brother takes the llamas home to your village.

Your eyes are wide as you enter the great city. There are many palaces of hewn stone, one story high. There are schools for the sons of nobles and great palaces where the rich live. But the greatest of all sights is the *Coricancha,* the house of gold. It is made of perfectly rectangular blocks of stone. A disc of solid gold in the middle represents the sun. The Villac Umu, high priest of the sun, is in charge. He is the second most important person in the empire. The most important, of course, is the emperor.

On the walls of the temple hang rich tapestries and massive ornaments of gold. There is even a garden of gold with life-sized stalks of maize (corn) cobs, animals, and birds.

You tell the grim-faced officials that you saw the man murder the warrior who tried to stop him. It turns out that the man was very rich to begin with. Great trust was put in him and he repaid it with dishonesty. He stole from the house of gold.

You know the laws of the Incas. If a commoner had done such a crime he would be fatally beaten with a club. Or maybe he would be thrown to his death off a great cliff. But you don't know what happens to a noble who commits such a crime.

You watch now to see what the sentence is.

"You shall be sent to the dungeon in the basement of the stone building in this city," says the judge.

You turn to a warrior and ask, "Is that a prison?"

The warrior shudders. "It is a special dungeon. It is filled with many passages leading to blind doors. There is no escape. Sharp points are in the floors and the walls. To walk upon them or fall into them is to be severely wounded. It is dark, and there in the darkness are pumas, jaguars, bears, and deadly snakes. Eventually the prisoner will be bitten or torn apart. It is the most loathsome fate a man can suffer. For the worst punishment is given to a person who has been given much and turns wicked anyway," says the warrior.

You head home from Cuzco then. You will never forget what you have seen here.

■ *Turn to page 169.*

You dash away into the crowd. Soon you are lost among the bobbing ponchos and baskets of the traders. You are afraid to go to Cuzco. You have heard rumors that when the emperor is sick, boys and girls about ten years old are killed and sacrificed to make the emperor well. You have heard of dungeons in Cuzco filled with snakes and wildcats.

You hurry back to your mountain village. You are glad when you see the thatched roofs of your village. Your brother is just ahead, leading the llamas.

The weather is very cold and you pull your poncho around your shoulders. You stoop to enter the low door to your home. There is no furniture in your house. You sit and sleep on grass mats on the floor.

The stone and mud stove is burning brightly. The smoke escapes through the thatch (brush) on your roof. The food you eat is almost always the same. It is soup or stew. Meat is rare. You sometimes eat the alpacas, but only when one is injured and cannot be a pack animal anymore. You eat maize, squash, and potatoes today. You will have some tomatoes as well. They will give your stew a better taste.

You are glad to eat the hot stew. You never complain. You have never lived any differently. Everyone you know lives the same. You believe it is right. You do not envy the rich nobles. They were born in that state. How could you be angry with them?

You enjoy the simple pleasures like a warm poncho and good hot stew. Sometimes there's a treat of broiled fish or duck. When you die, you are sure you will enjoy a good life in heaven. Until then, you love your mountain home. You enjoy sprinting over the wild mountain trails and counting the stars in the night skies. You think your life is very good.

■ *Turn to page 169.*

You decide to see what happens to the young thief. Your brother goes home with the llamas and you trail along with the warriors and their prisoner.

You travel to the landowner's farm, where the young serf and his family work and live. The warriors find all the serfs on this land living in great misery and hunger. The greedy landowner wants more profits than he deserves.

The warriors call the landowner outside and one of them says, "Landowner, you are fortunate in that you have much land. But it is your duty to be fair with your serfs. This young serf was caught stealing a tomato, for he was hungry. If he had stolen from greed he would be flogged. But he stole because he was hungry. Still, a crime was committed. A tomato was stolen. So somebody must be punished. You, greedy landholder, shall be flogged."

You are amazed and happy to see the landholder soundly whipped! You feel he will surely treat his serfs better from now on. If he mistreats them again he could be killed!

You arrive back in your mountain village just behind your brother. Already the smell of stew is coming from your hut. You are hungry and anxious to eat.

Just then you see a duck. How wonderful if you could add duck meat to your stew. You rarely enjoy meat. You grab your sling and hurl a stone at the duck. You bring down the wild duck and scramble into the rocks after it. It's a large, heavy bird. It will be tasty indeed!

The evening meal is very good. The hut is warm inside and you feel happy. You think how good it is to be a young Inca, strong and healthy, living in a beautiful mountaintop village.

■ *Turn to page 169.*

167 *Choosing Your Way Through the World's Medieval Past*

You don't want to see the young man punished. You feel sad enough. You and your brother hurry home with the alpacas.

As you walk, you see a team of shouting boys. They are all the sons of important officials. They are competing in a hard survival test. They are sent into the mountains without weapons or sandals. They must spend nine days in the wilderness. This will prove they are worthy young men.

You wonder if they will all survive. They have grown up in nice comfortable homes. They have had dainty food to eat. If they cannot find wild potatoes to eat, can they bear to do what you have done—eat snails and lizards?

You draw closer to home. You see smoke rising through the thatch of your roof. The evening meal is being made. The stew will taste much better when you add the tomatoes you have brought. But when you think of tomatoes you remember the poor young thief. Have they killed him yet for his theft? You feel so sad.

In the days ahead you think often of the young man. You wish you could forget him. But it was you who shouted "thief." Otherwise he would have gotten away with the tomato. A person should not have to die for being hungry and stealing a tomato.

One day you and your brother take your alpacas and go again to the marketplace.

"Look!" you cry out joyfully when you see the young man who stole your tomato. "He is alive."

"Let's go and ask him what happened," your brother says.

When you go to the young man, he smiles broadly. "The warriors did not punish me. They went to the landowner I work for. They found out how he cheats all his workers. So they whipped him! And now we are all treated much better. The landowner is afraid to cheat us anymore," he says.

You are so happy. Inca justice has worked well.

■ *Turn to page 169.*

Gift of the Incas

The Incas often suffered from a disease causing chills and fever. The Incas did not call the chills and fever malaria, but that's what it was. They discovered that by taking sticky gum from the bark of the cinchona tree they could help people who suffered from this illness. When Spanish priests came to Peru in the 1500's, they learned of this treatment. They spread the word, and all mankind had its first successful treatment for malaria. It was called quinine, and it reduced fever and pain from malaria.

Matching

_____ 1. Disease treated by the bark of the cinchona tree   a) quinine

_____ 2. Nationality of priests who came to Peru   b) vicuña

_____ 3. Pack animals of the Incas were alpaca and   c) malaria

_____ 4. Where Inca emperor lived   d) Cuzco

_____ 5. Medicine from the cinchona bark   e) Spanish

Group Activities

1. Discuss the Inca justice system. How was it fair or unfair? How did it compare to our system?

2. Look at a large map of South America and find the following:

Amazon River	Bolivia	Colombia
Andes Mountains	Paraguay	Ecuador
Peru	Chile	Venezuela
Brazil	Uruguay	Argentina

3. In Incan Peru you were born into a lower or upper class. How did this affect ambition, self-esteem (how people felt about themselves), and order in society? Discuss.

Individual Activities

1. Find pictures of alpaca, llama, and vicuña. Make a drawing of one and write one paragraph describing the animal.

2. The quipu was a series of knotted, colored strings tied to a main cord. It was used to figure arithmetic. Make a cord with several different-colored cords tied to it. Make knots in the colored cords.

3. Who rules Peru today? Find out the standard of living there and write a paragraph about life in Peru today.

A Renaissance Painter— 1450

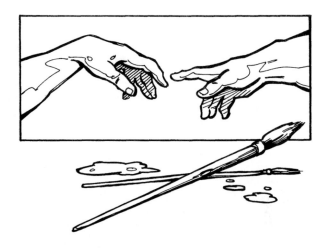

You are very young but already a talented painter in Italy. You are starting your career. You will make your living by selling your services to art patrons. These are wealthy people or important persons in the Church. You may be asked to paint portraits of members of wealthy families. Or you could be asked by a high churchman, like a cardinal or even the Pope, to paint a religious picture for a great cathedral. All you want to do is paint. This is the joy of your life. You hope to become rich and famous, too.

If you moved to Rome, you would have a good chance of being hired by a church official. St. Peter's, the most important Christian church in Italy, is there. If the Church became your patron you would have a bright future indeed. There are walls and ceilings of churches to be painted. You are very good at painting religious figures.

A very great painter and sculptor named Michelangelo has worked for the Pope for several years. It looks as if he may continue

to work for the Church all his life. What a fine future Michelangelo has!

If you would prefer to find a patron among the wealthy families of Italy, Florence would be the place to go. The Medici family of Florence is one of the most generous of them all. They patronize many artists. Botticelli and Ficino are two artists supported by the Medici family.

Where should you go—to Rome or Florence?

■ *If you go to Rome, turn to page 173.*

■ *If you go to Florence, turn to page 174.*

Find out what your fate is!

You decide you would have a better chance of being noticed in Rome. You hurry there and find the city filled with excitement over a new Pope. Nicholas V has just been elected and he plans many new projects. You are in luck!

Rome has suffered greatly in the past from wars and decay. Many of the churches are crumbling. The rain has even come in on the paved floors of St. Peter's. The Palatine hill is overrun with vegetation and even cattle roam there and in the old Roman Forum.

Now Pope Nicholas wants to repair everything! He is fixing aqueducts and building new fountains. He is repairing churches and bridges. Streets are being straightened and paved. The piles of filth and rubbish that have so long made Rome a sad place are to be cleaned up at last. And a brand new St. Peter's will be built!

What a time for a young artist to arrive in Rome. Fra Angelico has been hired to decorate the walls of the Vatican chapel with scenes of saints. You cannot hope for such a job. But maybe you might be hired to do a fresco (painting on wet, fresh plaster) somewhere in the Vatican.

When you have been in Rome for less than a month, a bishop offers you the chance to paint a Madonna (Virgin Mary) and Child on the wall of his private chapel.

But at the same time a wealthy family in Rome asks you to do portraits of their six children for their magnificent new villa.

"You have had more experience doing portraits of people," a friend reminds you.

This is true, but there is more prestige in doing the Madonna in the Vatican. Once you do work in the Vatican, many more opportunities may open up. Still, even the great Leonardo da Vinci painted portraits for prominent families. But what if your portraits do not prove flattering enough?

■ *If you do the fresco in the Vatican, turn to page 175.*

■ *If you do portraits for the wealthy family, turn to page 176.*

You decide you are more comfortable doing portraits, so you travel to Florence. You find that the Medici family dominates everything. You must somehow get their attention.

You make friends with other artists in Florence, and soon you are invited to a gathering at the Medici home in *Via Larga*. It seems that all the great artists of Europe are gathered here. You are very nervous as you prepare to meet the great Cosimo de Medici. If you make a good impression on him, your career could be on its way.

Cosimo de Medici is about 60 years old. He seems most gracious, and as you introduce yourself he smiles encouragingly. But then another, better-known artist barges into the conversation. He is already working for Cosimo de Medici. He leads him away and you are left speaking to the air!

Another wealthy man, though not nearly as famous as Cosimo de Medici, grabs your arm. "I understand you are a portrait artist," he says.

"Yes," you say eagerly.

"I wish to have a portrait of my beautiful daughter. She shall soon be having her eighteenth birthday and I must have a painter who will do her incredible beauty justice. Can you capture the beauty of a girl as wondrous as a fresh-blooming rose?" asks the man.

"Yes indeed," you say. You are very eager for a commission.

Soon the Florentine banker's carriage takes you to his great stone villa with stone flowers sculptured on the outside pillars. The daughter comes out to greet you.

You are surprised to find the daughter is not very beautiful. The way her father described her, you expected a great beauty.

How shall you paint her? You have heard she is kind and generous and a fine musician. Should you try to capture her inner beauty and paint her rather plain? Or would this upset her father? If you judge wrong and the father or daughter isn't pleased, your whole future could be ruined.

■ *If you paint the girl as a beauty, turn to page 177.*

■ *If you paint her realistically, turn to page 178.*

You decide to do the fresco. Your job is to paint the Christ Child on the lap of Mary. You ponder how to do this. It is the most important job of your life. If you do not please the bishop, you are in trouble. You know he and the Pope are good friends. The bishop will recommend you to the Pope for more work if you do well here.

Should you make Mary sweet and holy-looking in a very serious way? Should the Child be serious too—more like a saintly little adult than a chubby baby? You have seen many religious paintings like that.

You would like to follow your own heart, and that's what you end up doing. You begin sketching before you do the final painting. You make the Virgin Mary smiling warmly at the Baby. You make Jesus look like a real baby. He playfully tugs at his mother's hair just as real babies do. You have grown up in a large family and you know how babies are.

You sketch a warm family scene. Then you get an idea. You will show Joseph, too. He will be clearly amused by the baby's antics. You discover as you paint that you are painting the happiness you remember in your own family.

When you show the sketches to the bishop you are very nervous. You don't know what you'll do if he is not pleased. Maybe he is a very serious man without a sense of humor! Then you are doomed. "Here are my sketches of what the painting will look like," you say, "I will use rich, warm colors for the finished painting. It will look much more impressive than it does in these sketches. . . ."

The bishop looks puzzled. He grabs up your sketches. "I must show them to the Pope," he mutters.

He is gone a long time and your knees knock together. Then, at last, the bishop returns. He is smiling! "Pope Nicholas wants some like this for St. Peter's! The Pope, he is from a poor family you know, and he says the Holy Family looks very natural!"

You are on your way! You will be one of the great artists of the Renaissance!

■ *Turn to page 179.*

You travel to a villa in Rome where a marvelous garden surrounds the house. Laurel trees provide shade, and paths lead among streams, cascades, and pots filled with flowers. The wealthy owner walks with you. "I must have portraits of all members of my family. But first I must have a portrait of myself. Others have tried to capture my triumphant spirit, but they have failed. Can you do it?" asks the man.

You are very nervous. The fellow is not very handsome. He is tall and slender with a bald head. But if you pleased him, you could be set for life. He would spread the word of your artistry. "I believe I can do a fine job," you say.

You begin your portrait as the man sits in the garden. He has told you he has the strength of a lion and the spirit of an eagle. He wants these qualities to show in the portrait.

You stare at the plain, homely face and the shiny bald head as you work. You try very hard to make the man look strong and noble. You make the portrait as flattering as you can. Still, you are terrified when you must show him the results.

"Who is that silly pig?" screams the man.

You almost faint in terror. He is bright red with rage. He is almost jumping up and down. "But, you see," you stammer.

"You are no artist," the man shouts. "You have insulted me. Take that wretched portrait with you when you go!"

You barely escape the vase he throws after you. You make it out the door, but that's the least of your worries. The man is powerful. He tells everyone that you have no skill. You cannot get another commission.

You finally get work with a jeweler in Rome. You paint flowers on pretty little jewelry boxes. The money is very poor, but you make a living. It is not what you dreamed of, but it is better than nothing.

■ *Turn to page 179.*

The portrait you make is of a lovely maiden with lustrous brown curls, though the real girl's hair is thin, straight, and caught at her neck in a bun. You give her large, dark eyes with long lashes, though she has small pale eyes, rather close together. You give her rosy cheeks, though she is pale.

When the painting is finished, you unveil it for the father, mother, and daughter.

"It's beautiful," the father shouts. "What an artist you are! You have made our Lenore as lovely as she is."

"It's excellent," says the mother. "Oh, you are indeed an artistic genius!"

"Oh Father," says the girl with a laugh, "the painting is beautiful, but it's not me. You frightened the poor artist into painting an entirely different creature!"

The father scoffs at his daughter and pays you well. He promises to recommend you to many other wealthy patrons in the city.

But the daughter follows you out to the door. "Poor artist," she says, "How far you have strayed from the truth of your art!"

You get many other commissions in the city of Florence. You gain the reputation of making plain, even ugly, people beautiful. Families proudly hang dishonest portraits on their walls of less-than-attractive relatives.

You work constantly for the rich and the vain, but you are not very proud of what you do. Still, you live very well in your own beautiful villa. You will never be known as a great artist because everyone knows you are a flatterer. But you enjoy your money very much, and perhaps that will be enough for you.

■ *Turn to page 179.*

You see the inner goodness of the young woman, and you paint this in her gentle mouth, her luminous eyes. Still, you remain true to her facial features. Her sweet, plain face reveals the soul of a good and caring person.

But, you are very much afraid to show your work to her parents, especially her father. You did not deny your own artistic vision, but will the parents be pleased?

When you unveil the portrait, the father frowns. "Ugh. Lenore does not look like that. You have painted a homely girl. Lenore is beautiful."

"Yes," the mother agrees, "our daughter is a great beauty and you have painted a plain child."

"Nonsense," says the daughter with a smile. "The artist has tried to capture what is within me, and in so doing flatters me much more than words can say. I am so pleased that one could see goodness in me. I love the portrait. It will always be dear to me."

You are filled with gratitude. Although the parents refuse to recommend you to their wealthy friends, the girl introduces you to many important patrons in Florence. "This is a true artist with the ability to look deeper than flesh into the heart and soul of the subject," she says.

You gain many important patrons and each day your reputation grows. Your portraits have wonderful individual expressions that show insight into the character of those you paint. You are soon called the artist who paints souls.

You are called to Rome to do a portrait of the Pope. Pope Nicholas V has died and now Pius II reigns. After you paint his portrait he says, "You have made me an honest picture! It will hang in the Vatican as long as the world exists!"

Now you are ready to do great religious paintings. Your masterful biblical paintings will rank you among the giants of the Renaissance.

■ *Turn to page 179.*

Leonardo da Vinci

One of the greatest artists of the Renaissance was Leonardo da Vinci. He was a painter, sculptor, architect, and inventor. His scientific drawings of the human body and of machines not yet invented (like helicopters) amazed everybody. Leonardo loved to see how things worked. He drew a parachute before anybody ever thought of one. He also designed bridges and highways and weapons. His most famous painting is probably the *Mona Lisa*.

Matching

_____ 1. Wealthy people who supported artists were   a) Medici

_____ 2. This artist worked for the Pope   b) patrons

_____ 3. A prominent family in Florence   c) Leonardo

_____ 4. Botticelli and Ficino were   d) Michelangelo

_____ 5. Artist who made scientific sketches   e) painters of Florence

Group Activities

1. Discuss what artists had to do to make a living during the Renaissance. Is it harder or easier today to make a living as an artist?

2. Make posters displaying Renaissance art.

3. Leonardo designed weapons of war along with other inventions. Does this change your opinion of him? Why? Why not?

Individual Activities

1. Find and look at sketches by Leonardo. In one paragraph give your impressions of them.

2. Choose a Renaissance painter whose work you like and write a paragraph telling why you like it.

3. Choose one of the following and write one paragraph about the person:

   a) Raphael   b) Fra Angelico   c) Michelangelo

Over the Bounding Sea—1490

CHRISTOPHER COLUMBUS

You are a teenage sailor eager to see new lands across the ocean. You want to go where no Europeans have gone before. You must be on one of the exciting voyages being planned.

"But who knows what lies in the ocean?" says your sensible older brother. He is a cloth merchant. He is all grown up without any spirit of adventure left. You think he leads a very dull life. "There could be great sea serpents under the waves who would overturn your ship and devour you whole!"

"I have prepared for this adventure," you answer. "I've learned the art of sailing. I know all about the mariner's compass and the astrolabe that tells latitudes. I've sailed before. I'm not some ignorant person who is scared of sea serpents."

You have heard of a Portuguese noble named Vasco da Gama. He is not a brilliant man and some say he is harsh. But he is very brave and he plans an exciting sea voyage. He will leave for India in 1497. But that means you must wait seven years! In that time you must be content with shorter sea adventures. By 1497 you will be all grown up and maybe dull like your brother!

Another voyage will leave Palos, Spain, in less than two years. Christopher Columbus is an Italian seaman, but he has visited Portugal often. King Ferdinand and Queen Isabella of Spain are paying to send Columbus to find an ocean route to Asia. You have heard good things about Columbus. He is a fine man.

Friends tell you that Portuguese navigators like Vasco da Gama are more reliable at sea. But others say Columbus is a better natural sailor.

■ *If you go with Columbus, turn to page 183.*

■ *If you go with Vasco da Gama, turn to page 184.*

Find out what your fate is!

As you prepare to join Columbus on his voyage, a friend who is not as well educated as you says, "What if the earth is flat as some say? Won't your ships sail right off the edge into some awful emptiness?"

You smile and say, "Oh, the earth is a sphere. And there is land at the western end of the Atlantic. We are sure of it."

Your friend shakes his head in wonder. And you are off to Palos, Spain, where the expedition is organizing.

On August 3, 1492, three ships, the *Niña,* the *Pinta,* and the *Santa Maria,* leave. You are among the 90 sailors aboard the *Pinta.*

After a short time at sea, you stop at the Canary Islands to make repairs and take on fresh food. Then you head out across the Atlantic.

After many days at sea, many of the sailors feel they are in the middle of an endless sea. None of you has ever been so far from land before.

"Do you think Columbus knows where he's going?" whispers a fearful sailor. "Or are we lost?"

"We seem to be moving in great circles," his companion mutters. "I fear we shall all die of hunger and thirst. We shall never escape this wretched sea."

"Let us seize the foolish captain and take over the ship," says the first sailor.

"No, no, we must trust Columbus," you insist.

At 2 A.M. on October 12, everybody is shouting "Land!" With screams of joy and relief you go ashore. You find beautiful hills and many palm trees. There are lovely fruit trees and soft, grassy meadows. Even the native people are friendly.

One day, as you explore on your own, a native comes from the brush. He wants to trade his golden ornament for your old leather strap. It's not a fair trade, but you would like that ornament.

■ *If you make the trade, turn to page 185.*

■ *If not, turn to page 186.*

You wait a long time to make your great voyage, but you gain a lot of valuable experience at sea. You feel you are better prepared for the longest journey of your life now.

In July of 1497, Vasco da Gama sails off in four ships with 150 sailors. You are among them. You leave Lisbon and sail directly into the south Atlantic sea.

"How daring the captain is," says a fellow seaman. "Most would keep land in sight as long as possible. But Vasco da Gama goes right into the open sea!"

Your captain is truly fearless. But he is cruel, too. No sailor dares disobey him, for the sailor is harshly punished for it. Maybe that's the way it has to be on the high seas, you think.

You see no land for three months and you are running short of food. Scurvy, a disease that comes from lack of vitamin C, breaks out among the sailors. You get it, too. Your gums bleed and you feel very weak. Worse yet, you must fight savage winds and high seas as you sail around the Cape of Good Hope in Africa. You fear drowning, but half the time you are so sick you don't even care what happens to you.

At last you are sailing up the east coast of Africa. You drop anchor there and trade for oranges, lemons, and sugar cane. How good it is to eat fresh fruit. Your strength slowly returns.

Finally, in May of 1498, you reach India. You are greeted coldly by the Indians. You are dressed in heavy leather and woolen pants. The Indians wear cool cotton. They think you are strange people to be dressed so heavily.

But when Vasco da Gama offers the Indians gifts of striped cloth, strings of coral, and some wash basins, they are really insulted! They have beautiful clothing and luxuries. They seem more civilized than you are.

Maybe you should slip away from Vasco da Gama before he turns the Indians against the whole expedition!

■ *If you slip away on your own, turn to page 187.*

■ *If you remain with Vasco da Gama, turn to page 188.*

The golden ornament glitters so beautifully. And the native fellow has no use for it. He really wants your leather strap. So you make the trade.

Suddenly, there is Columbus looking very stern. "You there," he says, seeing the ornament in your hand, "where did you get that?"

"A native man traded it to me," you explain. "Just a moment ago he made the trade, and then took the leather strap very gladly and hurried away."

You can tell that Columbus is not pleased. He scowls fiercely. "These poor native people are so easily robbed. They will give objects of great value for trifles. One of my sailors traded a few broken dishes for 30 pounds of cotton. I will not have such cheating going on, do you understand?"

Feeling ashamed, you hurry into the brush and find the native. You give him back his ornament. (Maybe it isn't real gold anyway!) But you let him keep the old leather strap.

You begin searching for gold here, but you find none. If the ornaments are made of gold, the native people must have traded them with others from distant lands.

You set sail with Columbus and reach another island (Cuba). When no gold is found there, you continue on to a third island, which Columbus names Hispaniola (now Haiti and the Dominican Republic).

In January of 1493 Columbus sets sail for home. You never regained the full trust of Columbus when he thought you had cheated the native. So you decide to remain behind at the settlement of La Navidad. You would like more time to look for gold anyway. When Columbus returns again, he will find you rich; then maybe he will forget you tried to cheat the native man.

But when Columbus returns six months later, he finds the settlement in ruins. You and 38 others are dead. You fought among yourselves and you fought the native people. Most of the 39 died violently, but you drowned while trying to spear a fish.

■ *Turn to page 189.*

You feel bad about taking the native's beautiful ornament. It just isn't fair. So you give him the leather strap he wants so much in exchange for a bird feather he has. That is a more even trade. The native is delighted. You have made a friend.

Columbus has seen the incident. Now he comes forward smiling. He claps you on the shoulder. "Some of my sailors have tried to cheat the natives. God bless you for being honest. You will go far in this world, and in the world beyond where people are judged for their lives."

You sail with Columbus to another island (Cuba) and then to a third, which Columbus names Hispaniola (now Haiti and the Dominican Republic).

After some time you return to Spain with Columbus, leaving behind 39 men at a settlement which Columbus called La Navidad. Then, six months later, you go on another voyage to the New World with him. You reach the island he named Hispaniola, and find La Navidad destroyed. Columbus starts a new settlement there and he asks you to help govern it!

By 1509, Columbus's son, Diego, is governor of Hispaniola and you are his trusted assistant. Then, later, you become a governor yourself in Cuba. You gain a large amount of land.

You build a find home on your great estate in Cuba. It is like a medieval castle. You have a winding staircase and a beautiful view of the sea. Your life is far better than you imagined it could be. Your walls are covered with tapestries which you have brought from Spain. Your floors are made of gleaming Spanish tile.

You journey back to Europe and marry, and bring your spouse to your beautiful home in Cuba. Soon you are raising children. Your sugar cane crop thrives. You have lush gardens and you are at home in the New World.

The native people you respected when you arrived here have become your farm laborers. Some must be forced to work and you are sorry about that. But what else can you do? You certainly can't do all the work yourself.

You console yourself by reminding yourself that you are kind to your workers.

■ *Turn to page 189.*

You are sure that Vasco da Gama or some of the others in your party will insult and enrage the Indians and there will be trouble. So you leave the expedition. You are glad you did, because soon Vasco da Gama is in a bitter fight with some Arab merchants who control the trade routes around here.

You travel overland across Africa with a band of merchants. After a long and difficult journey, you reach Spain. But your appetite for adventure is not gone. You sail to Hispaniola in the New World, and in a few years you join Hernando Cortés on an expedition to Mexico.

You march with Cortés toward the Aztec empire at Tenochtitlán. What a splendid city it is. Aqueducts carry fresh water. The city is filled with canals, and the palaces and temples are filled with gold and silver statues. But some of what you see is not so beautiful.

At the temple at Tenochtitlán you see many human skulls. Thousands of people, often captives from war, have been sacrificed here.

At first Cortés makes peace with the Aztec leader Montezuma. But soon war breaks out. You are outnumbered by the Aztecs. You flee with Cortés until fresh soldiers come. In 1521, you defeat the Aztecs. The city of Tenochtitlán is burned to the ground.

You watch the magnificent city in flames and you have mixed feelings. You are glad you have won a victory. But you are sad at the high cost.

Suddenly you see Hernando Cortés. He is standing alone watching the city burn, too. You walk to his side. In a soft voice he says, "I had hoped to save the city." He is near tears. You are, too. Too many wonderful buildings with remarkable treasures have been destroyed. But much worse than that, to make the victory possible, too many people have died.

■ *Turn to page 189.*

You remain with Vasco da Gama and join him when he meets the ruler of this part of India.

The Indian ruler wears a jeweled collar, jeweled anklets, and beautiful rings on his fingers. Vasco da Gama offers him more cheap trinkets and he laughs. But the Arab merchants who control the trade in India do not laugh when they meet Vasco da Gama. They demand that he leave at once.

"All trade from India and Europe is conducted by Arab merchants," one Arab tells you. "For years we have brought the spices and precious stones from India to Europe. It shall always be so."

Vasco da Gama has a meeting with all his sailors. "We must slip spices and jewels aboard our ship. Then we will take this to Europe. We shall make a huge profit. We will not have to share the profit with the Arabs, so the prices can be lower and more will be sold. Once we are successful in one journey, we can do the same all the time. We will have broken the Arab control on trade to and from India," he says.

You and the other sailors travel around the Indian city buying spices and jewels. You buy ginger, cinnamon, cloves, nutmeg, and pepper. Another sailor brings jeweled finger and toe rings. You sneak these things aboard the ship at night. Soon you shall sail for home and a great deal of money.

You breathe a sigh of relief when you are at sea. You have outsmarted the Arab merchants.

But on the journey home there is a disaster you never dreamed of. Your ships are becalmed at sea. There is not enough wind to fill your sails. For days on end you sit in the middle of the water. You run out of fresh fruits and vegetables. Scurvy, a disease that comes from lack of vitamin C, breaks out among the sailors.

Your gums are spongy and bleeding. You are too weak even to stand. Eating bread or anything is too painful to endure. Each day you hope for wind. It's a hellish ordeal.

Many of Vasco da Gama's sailors die and are buried at sea. You are one of them.

■ *Turn to page 189.*

Sailing to the New World

In the 1400's a new kind of ship sailed to the New World. They were caravels, weighing from 75 to 200 tons. They had square sails. The hull was sturdy enough to endure the high ocean waves. The caravels traveled about 12 miles per hour. Forty sailors could fit on such ships. The sailors had simple food—codfish, beans, and hardtack bread. These foods could be stored for a long time. But the sailors also needed fresh fruit and vegetables and these could not be stored. So, although high winds and waves destroyed many ships, scurvy was probably the sailors' worst enemy. If the sea journey was too long, or the winds becalmed a ship, the terrible disease took a large toll of sailors.

Matching

_____ 1. The instrument which tells latitude   a) Italian

_____ 2. Nationality of Vasco da Gama   b) Portuguese

_____ 3. Vasco da Gama's voyage left from   c) caravels

_____ 4. Nationality of Columbus   d) astrolabe

_____ 5. The sturdy new ships explorers used   e) Portugal

Group Activities

1. On a large map find the voyages of Magellan, Columbus, Hudson, Cabral, the Cabots, and Verrazano.

2. Make a large poster of a caravel, or a model ship such as those used by the explorers.

3. Discuss European exploration to the New World. What would North and South America be like today if the explorers had not come? Do you think it was inevitable (certain) that somebody would have come from Europe to settle the New World?

Individual Activities

1. Find information about one of the following and write a paragraph about him.

   a) Magellan   b) Hudson   c) Cabral

2. Draw a compass and an astrolabe.

3. Find maps showing how people thought the world looked in the 1400's. In two paragraphs describe some major mistakes these early map makers made.

Faith and Land—1524

MARTIN LUTHER

You are a young peasant in Germany. You must still rent land from a lord. You have no right to hunt in the woodland or even fish in the streams. Your family eats meager food, often just dry bread and a little cheese. The only meat you might have would be wild game, but the lord alone may hunt around here.

"Look at him up there in his great castle," you say bitterly. "The pride and cruelty of that wicked fellow. I cannot stand it much longer."

Your spouse agrees. "He lives in great luxury. Why, he will eat half a deer at one meal and throw leftover venison to his dogs. We do not eat as well as the dogs under his table!"

"This preacher," you say, "Martin Luther. He speaks of these injustices. He says that all people must be equal. He says we peasants must not be trodden down under the feet of princes and lords."

Your spouse nods. "I like what he says. We get no help from the state. And the bishop does not help us either. It seems everyone is against the peasant."

You belong to a peasants' group. You meet nights and write demands for the free use of forest and stream. The local parish priest is on your side. But the local bishop is from a wealthy family. He is on the side of the lord.

Tonight at the meeting a neighbor says, "I like what Luther says about the poor. But I don't agree with his new religious ideas."

Your own family is not very religious. You go to the Catholic church. But you don't understand the religious arguments that are flaring around you. You just want a better life for you and your family.

"Enough talk!" a man shouts. "I'm for burning down the landlord's house tonight. Who is brave enough to join me?"

■ *If you go with the man, turn to page 193.*

■ *If not, turn to page 194.*

Find out what your fate is!

You have suffered too much to continue begging for justice. You and some other angry young peasants arm yourselves for the fight ahead. You are sick of being hungry. You are sick of having no future.

One dark night you and the others climb the hill to your landlord's great house. You wear scarves to hide your faces. The lord is shocked to see you coming. He rushes away with his family as you break down the door.

What a beautiful house this is! There are rich tapestries on the wall. You rip them down and set fire to them. You laugh and scream in glee. You are letting out all the hatred you have long felt. You snatch up money and jewelry. Then you overturn the furniture and hurl it into the raging fire. You take special joy in ripping down a portrait of the lord and pitching that into the fire, too.

You leave the blazing inferno, singing and shouting.

"This is only the beginning," cries your leader. "We shall crush all the princes who have ruined our lives. We will pull down the high churchmen who have not defended our cause. Everyone must be equal. We must share everything equally as they did in the time of the early Christians."

"Martin Luther himself has said our cause is just," you shout. You get into the spirit of the violent night. "He says the evil princes deserve to be thrown out, for they have caused our misery."

But then the man beside you looks worried. He is better educated than you are. He says, "Luther also said that violence was never allowable. I do not think he would approve of what we did tonight."

You stand at the bottom of the hill and smile at the flames leaping into the black night sky. What a glorious sight. You have looked up that hill often in bitter envy. Now you laugh and howl.

"Let's do some more burning!" shouts your leader.

You aren't sure you want that. You are eager to go home now and see what happens. Maybe this one act of violence will bring you justice.

■ *If you stay with the violent peasants, turn to page 195.*

■ *If you go home, turn to page 196.*

You write a document called the *Twelve Articles* listing your demands for justice. You ask that peasants be allowed to hunt and fish anywhere. This would help a lot. You demand a reduction in the work you owe your landlord. Often you are so busy working for him that you have no time for your own farmland. You demand a fair wage for your labor. You ask that the rent you pay for your farmland be fair and just. Then you and some of your neighbors sign the document.

Martin Luther likes your document. He writes a pamphlet agreeing with your demands, but he warns against violence. No matter what your grievances are, he warns, it is never right to resort to violence. This makes some of the peasants angry.

"If they pay no attention to these written demands, then we'll see what we have to do," you say.

The next day your neighbor decides that he will not wait to see if the *Twelve Articles* do any good. He attacks and beats his landlord. The landlord is a wicked man and the poor peasant's children are weak with hunger. You hardly blame him for what he did, but you are frightened. What will happen now?

Martin Luther issues a new pamphlet. He denounces violence in even stronger terms. He seems to be afraid a bloody revolution will soon break out in Germany.

"Luther has turned against us," your spouse grumbles.

You are very confused. You don't know what to think. You go down to the parish church to see the priest. He is as poor and ragged as you are. He always has a coin for you, though. He keeps a poor box into which rich people sometimes put money because they are afraid of going to hell when they die. From this box, the priest doles out coins.

"What can I do?" you ask the priest.

"Why not go into town and try to earn a little money? There is nothing but starvation on the farm," he says.

You hate to leave the farm where you have always lived.

■ *If you go into town, turn to page 197.*

■ *If you remain on the farm, turn to page 198.*

The violent members of your group have convinced you that this is the only way to get attention. You attack the houses of other landlords and even hurl a stone through the bishop's house. You smash his front window!

"All princes must be put to the sword," cries your leader.

But now the tide turns against you. The princes are raising armies to attack the peasant warriors. Professional soldiers march against you. Your loosely organized peasant army is no match for regular soldiers with the newest weapons!

You barely survive the autumn of 1525. Most of your neighbors have been killed in bitter battles with regular soldiers.

"We were fools to turn to violence," you tell your spouse. You pack your few possessions and, with your spouse and children, flee into the Swabian forest. You are a hunted person and you must live like an animal for several months. You eat wild berries and fish from the streams.

When the violence ends, you travel to the German town of Münster. You join a new religion. The Anabaptists study the Bible and sing sad songs about the suffering of life. One of them lets you work in his bakery. You make enough to survive.

By now there are bitter religious wars going on all over Europe. It seems that nobody likes anybody else. The Catholics don't like the Lutherans. The Lutherans don't like the Catholics. And nobody likes the Anabaptists. So most of the time you must hide your beliefs. Many people think Anabaptists are violent revolutionaries. So you hide and read your Bible in secret by candlelight.

You hope that someday people can live in peace and friendship no matter what church or temple they go to. You hope that the economic life is fair, too. But none of this happens in your lifetime.

You spend your life eking out a living as a baker's helper and not telling anybody who is a stranger what faith you follow.

■ *Turn to page 199.*

You have had enough violence for one night. You hurry home to your farm. You hope the burning of the landlord's house scares the rich people into giving the peasants more rights. But that is not what happens. Soon the landlords and the princes hire armies to protect their property. They crush any peasants who rise up against them. You do not have the courage to continue the fight. Or maybe it would be just foolish to do so. Luckily nobody knows of your one violent act.

You struggle along on your farm with no hope in sight. And then one day your parish priest notices that your son has musical talent. The priest somehow finds the money to send your son to a music teacher.

Your son's beautiful singing voice is a miracle for your family. The boy's talent allows him to travel all over Europe singing for princes and merchants and even high churchmen. You and your spouse and son and daughter go to Sicily and Milan in Italy.

"The boy has the voice of an angel," says one choir master.

When your son grows up, he moves to Antwerp. He has enough money to help you move there, too. The boy has outgrown his boyish soprano voice, but now he is a fine tenor. He can earn good money singing at the opera and giving concerts.

You have a nice home in Antwerp and you feel very lucky. Your friends and neighbors in Germany could not escape the tragedy of their lives. How lucky you are!

But the bitter religious differences of this period strike your new city of Antwerp with great force. People with strange new ideas are everywhere. Here a man says that everyone is evil. Here a man says that all governments must be overthrown. The people who were your new friends are accusing each other of being dangerous heretics, people who do not agree with a religious dogma.

You don't say much of anything to anybody. You are Catholic, but you never discuss it with strangers. You just go about your business and hope things get better soon.

■ *Turn to page 199.*

■ *Turn to page 199.*

You go to a nearby town with your spouse and two children. You must share a dirty, crowded house with two other families. Your son takes ill and dies in the first winter. Now you, your spouse, and daughter must look for menial labor anywhere you can find it.

Prices are rising so high you can hardly buy food. There are few jobs and those that exist pay so very little.

Your young daughter enters a convent and your spouse dies and you are now all alone. You are nothing more than a wandering beggar. You lie down in a field and wish you could die at once. But then you hear a man groaning.

You can hardly believe it, but the fellow is worse off than you. He is lame and half blind. He has not eaten in four days. You must do something for him. You carry the man to a monastery at the edge of town. "Here, take this poor fellow and give him a clean place to die," you say. Then, before waiting for the monk to speak, you turn to go.

"We have work here," says the monk.

"Work?" you ask. "I can neither write well nor do any skilled work. What use would I be?"

"For one thing we need someone to help us bury the dead," says the monk. "Many die in the streets. There is no one to bury them. Don't you think a person should at least be buried?"

You decide to stay at the monastery. At least you will have enough to eat and a place to sleep out of the weather.

You spend most of your time digging graves for poor people who have died alone. Once in a while you find a dying person and bring him or her to the monastery in time.

"Once I had hopes for a good life," you tell one of the monks. "I have lost my spouse, my farm, everything."

The monk smiles and says, "You are doing good work now. Burying the dead is a work of mercy."

You go on working at the monastery. Now you help the poor and the sick at the infirmary (hospital). You make friends of some of these poor, downtrodden people. Why not? You are one of them.

■ *Turn to page 199.*

You remain on the farm. You are afraid to do anything else. One day you hear your young son singing.

"What a beautiful voice he has," your spouse says.

You are feeling very bitter. "He is a fool. Why does he sing when we haven't bread enough to eat?" you say. You go to your son and shout, "Idiot! Don't you know we are starving? We have a few potatoes in the house. It has been weeks since we had meat. What do you sing for?"

"I sing because I must," the boy says.

You grow even angrier. "Do you see my crops dying in the fields? Do you think my heartless landlord will take pity and reduce the rent? Never! If I hear your foolish singing any longer, I will whip you!"

The boy looks very sad. You have made him ashamed to sing. He doesn't raise his voice in song anymore. And he never tells you about his secret dream, to sing in public. He works in the fields, but he does not sing anymore as he used to. He does not even smile anymore either.

You feel sorry that you lost your temper with your son. But he must be made to see how brutal and hard life is. How will he make his way in the world if he is a fool?

A bloody peasant revolt breaks out and life grows even worse. Many farms are burned by the armies that sweep across Germany.

One day the parish priest comes to visit. He asks you where your son is. "I miss him in the choir. Such a beautiful voice he has. I am trying to arrange for him to have music lessons. If his voice were well trained he might have a good future in music."

"My son has gone to join the army," you say sadly. "He went only a few weeks ago."

"Ah," says the priest, shaking his head sadly.

"He did not sing much anymore anyway," your spouse says.

That night you weep in your bed.

■ *Turn to page 199.*

■ *Turn to page 199.*

Books

In 1440 Johann Gutenberg invented a printing system. His first book was a Bible. That book is now the most valuable book in the world because it was the first that Gutenberg's system produced. Soon books of all kinds were coming off the printing presses. Before this, there was little reason for people to learn to read and write. Most people never even saw a book. They didn't need to read signs because stores showed the products they sold in pictures. For example, a shoemaker had a picture of shoes on his sign. Now, suddenly, ordinary people could actually see a book. They could own a book. Knowledge was increased. The world was changed forever.

Matching

_____ 1. Peasants in Germany were forbidden to   a) Bible

_____ 2. He said all men were equal.   b) hunt and fish

_____ 3. The first book printed in 1440   c) read and write

_____ 4. Inventor of printing system   d) Johann Gutenberg

_____ 5. Before 1440 there was little reason to learn to   e) Martin Luther

Group Activities

1. Look at a map of Europe. Find the countries that remained mostly Catholic and those that became Protestant in this period.

2. The central issue for the German peasants was to suffer in nonviolent patience or to start a revolution. Discuss the advantages and disadvantages of both courses of action.

3. In some of the selections, lack of religious freedom caused great trouble. Discuss the importance of religious freedom and freedom of thought in general.

Individual Activities

1. Find information about one of the following people from the Protestant Reformation. Write a paragraph about him.

   a) Martin Luther   b) John Calvin   c) John Knox

2. Find a photograph of a page from the Gutenberg Bible. In one paragraph describe it.

3. Imagine you have been asked to write an argument for or against violent revolution. In one or two paragraphs write your opinion.

Answer Key

1. A Germanic Villager

1. b   4. d
2. e   5. c
3. a

2. The Girl Who Became an Empress

1. c   4. e
2. b   5. d
3. a

3. A Mayan Adventure

1. c   4. b
2. a   5. d
3. e

4. When Charlemagne Ruled

1. d   4. b
2. a   5. c
3. e

5. Life in the Golden Age of China

1. b   4. d
2. e   5. a
3. c

6. Life in an English Castle

1. T   4. F
2. T   5. F
3. F

7. Upon the Viking Sea

1. d   4. b
2. e   5. c
3. a

8. Bazaars of Baghdad

1. F   4. T
2. T   5. F
3. F

9. In Robin Hood's Time

1. d   4. a
2. c   5. b
3. e

10. A Life of Service

1. c   4. e
2. d   5. b
3. a

11. Sunday in London

1. d   4. c
2. e   5. a
3. b

12. When Great Adventure Called

1. F   4. T
2. F   5. F
3. T

13. Samurai Decision

1. c   4. b
2. e   5. a
3. d

14. Medieval Craftsperson

1. T   4. T
2. T   5. F
3. F

15. In the Empire of Mali

1. e   4. c
2. d   5. b
3. a

16. The Grim Reaper

1. T   4. T
2. T   5. F
3. F

17. The Inca Way

1. c   4. d
2. e   5. a
3. b

18. A Renaissance Painter

1. b   4. e
2. d   5. c
3. a

19. Over the Bounding Sea

1. d   4. a
2. b   5. c
3. e

20. Faith and Land

1. b   4. d
2. e   5. c
3. a

Bibliography

1. A Germanic Villager

Heer, Friedrich. *The Medieval World*. Cleveland: World Publishing Co., 1962.

Hoyt, Robert S. *Europe in the Middle Ages*. New York: Harcourt, Brace & World, 1957 (pp. 1–42).

Lunt, W.E. *History of England*. New York: Harper & Brothers, 1957 (pp. 21–80).

2. The Girl Who Became an Empress

Hoyt, Robert S. *Europe in the Middle Ages*. New York: Harcourt, Brace & World, 1957 (pp. 103–5).

Jacobs, David, ed., and the editors of *Horizon Magazine*. *Constantinople: City on the Golden Horn*. New York: Harper & Brothers, 1969.

"Procopius, History of the Wars and Secret Histories: Justinian and the Foundations of the Byzantine Empire." *The Development of Civilization*, Vol. I. Chicago: Scott, Foresman & Co., 1961 (pp. 203–9).

3. A Mayan Adventure

Josephy, Alvin M., Jr. *The Indian Heritage of America*. New York: Bantam, 1968 (pp. 200–8).

"Life in the New World without Iron, Horses or Ploughs." *The Last Two Million Years*. Reader's Digest History of Man. New York: The Reader's Digest Association, 1973 (pp. 190–3).

Morley, Sylvanus G., and George W. Brainerd. *The Ancient Maya*. Stanford: Stanford University Press, 1983.

Rothenberg, Jerome. *Shaking the Pumpkin*. New York: Doubleday, 1972 (pp. 295–6).

Simpson, Lesley Byrd. *Many Mexicos*. Berkeley: University of California Press, 1964 (pp. 1–19).

4. When Carlemagne Ruled

"Einhard, Life of Charlemagne: The Carolingian Empire of the Franks." *The Development of Civilization*, Vol. I. Chicago: Scott, Foresman & Co., 1961 (pp. 256–60).

Heer, Friedrich. *Charlemagne and His World*. New York: Macmillan, 1975.

Hoyt, Robert S. *Europe in the Middle Ages*. New York: Harcourt, Brace & World, 1957 (pp. 125–58).

Komroff, Manuel. *Charlemagne*. New York: Mulian Messner, 1964.

Sayers, Dorothy L. *The Song of Roland*. New York: Penguin, 1985.

5. Life in the Golden Age of China

"The Ageless Mystery of China." *The Last Two Million Years.* Reader's Digest History of Man. New York: The Reader's Digest Association, 1973 (pp. 168–79).

Lum, Peter. *Six Centuries in East Asia.* New York: S.G. Phillips, 1973.

McNeill, William H. *A World History.* New York: Oxford University Press, 1967 (pp. 216–32).

Morton, William Scott. *China: Its History and Culture.* New York: Lippincott and Crowell, 1980.

Smith, Huston. *The Religions of Man.* New York: A Mentor Book, 1962 (pp. 90–150).

6. Life in an English Castle

Brooks, Polly Schoyer, and Nancy Zinsser Walworth. *The World of Walls: The Middle Ages in Western Europe.* New York: Lippincott, 1966.

Brown, Allen. *Castles: A History and Guide.* Blandford, Great Britain: Blandford Press, 1981.

Hoyt, Robert S. *Europe in the Middle Ages.* New York: Harcourt, Brace & World, 1957 (pp. 292–7).

Lunt, W.E. *History of England.* New York: Harper & Brothers, 1957 (pp. 80, 95, 104–24).

Warner, Philip. *The Medieval Castle.* New York: Taplinger Publishing Co., 1971.

7. Upon the Viking Sea

Chubb, Thomas C. *The Northmen.* Cleveland: World Publishing Co., 1964.

Donovan, Frank R., and the editors of *Horizon Magazine. The Vikings.* New York: Harper & Brothers, 1964.

Lunt, W.E. *The History of England.* New York: Harper & Brothers, 1957 (pp. 42–3, 51–4).

Poertner, Rudolf. *The Vikings: The Rise and Fall of the Norse Sea Kings.* New York: St. Martin's Press, 1975.

8. Bazaars of Baghdad

"An Empire Built in the Name of Allah." *The Last Two Million Years.* Reader's Digest History of Man. New York: The Reader's Digest Association, 1973 (pp. 148–57).

"Islam." *The Development of Civilization,* Vol. I. Chicago: Scott, Foresman & Co., 1961 (pp. 227–46).

Lippman, Thomas W. *Understanding Islam: An Introduction to the Moslem World.* New York: New American Library, 1982.

Stewart, Desmond, and the editors of *Life Magazine. The Arab World.* New York: Time-Life Books, 1962.

9. In Robin Hood's Time

Green, Roger Lancelyn. *The Adventures of Robin Hood.* New York: Puffin Books, 1956.

Hilton, R.H., ed. *Peasants, Knights and Heretics: Studies in Medieval English Social History.* Cambridge: Cambridge University Press, 1976.

Lunt, W.E. *The History of England.* New York: Harper & Brothers, 1957 (pp. 80–205).

10. A Life of Service

Chesterton, G.K. *St. Francis of Assisi.* New York: Doubleday, 1957.

Hopper, Vincent F., and Gerald B. Lahey, eds. *Medieval Mysteries and Moralities and Interludes.* Great Neck, N.Y.: Barron's Educational Series, Inc., 1962.

11. Sunday in London

Carter, Avis Murton. *One Day in Shakespeare's England.* New York: Abelard-Schuman Ltd., 1974.

"William Fitz Stephen: A Description of the Most Noble City of London." *The Development of Civilization,* Vol. I. Chicago: Scott, Foresman & Co., 1961 (pp. 271–4).

12. When Great Adventure Called

Bokenkotter, Thomas. *A Concise History of the Catholic Church.* New York: Doubleday, 1977 (pp. 136–7, 151–3).

"Crusades to Rescue the Holy Land from Islam." *The Last Two Million Years.* Reader's Digest History of Man. New York: The Reader's Digest Association, 1973 (pp. 220–1).

Lathan, Ronald, ed. *The Travels of Marco Polo.* Baltimore: Penguin Books, 1959.

Rugoff, Milton L., Carrington Goodrich, and the editors of *Horizon Magazine. Marco Polo's Adventures in China.* New York: Harper & Row, 1964.

13. Samurai Decision

"Artistry amid Violence: The Enigma of Japan." *The Last Two Million Years.* Reader's Digest History of Man. New York: The Reader's Digest Association, 1973 (pp. 184–7).

Hane, Mikiso. *Japan: A Historical Survey.* New York: Scribner's, 1972.

"Japan." *The Development of Civilization,* Vol. I. Chicago: Scott, Foresman & Co., 1961 (pp. 514–32).

McNeill, William H. *A World History.* New York: Oxford University Press, 1967 (pp. 264–7).

Meyer, Milton Walter. *Japan: A Concise History.* Littlefield, Adams, 1976.

14. Medieval Craftsperson   Hopper, Vincent, and Gerald B. Lahey, eds. *Medieval Mysteries and Moralities and Interludes.* Great Neck, N.Y.: Barron's Educational Series, Inc., 1962 (pp. 1–68, 147–95).

Hoyt, Robert S. *Europe in the Middle Ages.* New York: Harcourt, Brace & World, 1957 (pp. 429–35).

Lunt, W.E. *The History of England.* New York: Harper & Brothers, 1957 (pp. 172–89).

Snyder, James. *Medieval Art.* New York: Prentice-Hall, 1989.

15. In the Empire of Mali   Adams, Russell L. *Great Negroes Past and Present.* Chicago: Afro-American Publishing Co., Inc., 1969 (pp. 1–7).

de Blij, Harm J. *A Geography of Subsaharan Africa.* Chicago: Rand McNally, 1964 (pp. 49–53).

"Early Kingdoms of Tropical Africa." *The Last Two Million Years.* Reader's Digest History of Man. New York: The Reader's Digest Association, 1973 (pp. 204–11).

16. The Grim Reaper   "All Fall Dead." *Strange Stories—Amazing Facts.* New York: The Reader's Digest Association, 1976 (p. 55).

Gottfried, Robert S. *The Black Death.* London: Collier Macmillan, 1983.

Hoyt, Robert S. *Europe in the Middle Ages.* New York: Harcourt, Brace & World, 1957 (pp. 526–7, 575–7).

Lunt, W.E. *The History of England.* New York: Harper & Brothers, 1957 (pp. 237–40).

17. The Inca Way   Bailey, Helen Miller, and Abraham P. Nasatir. *Latin America.* New Jersey: Prentice-Hall, 1960 (pp. 77–86).

Bingham, Hiram. *The Lost City of the Incas.* New York: Atheneum, 1986.

Herring, Hubert. *A History of Latin America.* New York: Alfred A. Knopf, 1961 (pp. 47–55).

Josephy, Alvin M., Jr. *The Indian Heritage of America.* New York: Bantam, 1968 (pp. 2, 34, 245–6, 247–8).

18. A Renaissance Painter

Furguson, Wallace K., et al., eds. *The Renaissance.* New York: Harper Torchbooks, 1953 (pp. 123–82).

Gardner, Helen. *Art Through the Ages.* New York: Harcourt, Brace & World, 1959 (pp. 292–394).

Lucas, Henry S. *The Renaissance and the Reformation.* New York: Harper & Brothers, 1960.

Ralph, Philip Lee. *The Renaissance in Perspective.* New York: St. Martin's Press, 1973.

19. Over the Bounding Sea

Herring, Hubert. *A History of Latin America.* New York: Alfred A. Knopf, 1961 (pp. 121–7).

Humble, Richard. *The Explorers.* New York: Time-Life Books, 1978.

"Journal of the First Voyage of Vasco da Gama: Passage to India." *The Development of Civilization,* Vol. I. Chicago: Scott, Foresman & Co., 1961 (pp. 392–8).

Lucas, Henry S. *The Renaissance and the Reformation.* New York: Harper & Brothers, 1960 (pp. 376–88).

20. Faith and Land

Bainton, Roland Herbert. *The Reformation of the 16th Century.* Boston: Beacon Press, 1985.

Lucas, Henry S. *The Renaissance and the Reformation.* New York: Harper & Brothers, 1960 (pp. 569–80).

Marty, Martin E. *A Short History of Christianity.* Cleveland: Meridian Books, 1963 (pp. 207–18).